# THE SOUTH BUILDS

# THE SOUTH BUILDS

## New Architecture in the Old South

by EDWARD WAUGH, A.I.A., A.R.I.B.A.
AND
ELIZABETH WAUGH

with HENRY L. KAMPHOEFNER, F.A.I.A., *Advisor*

Chapel Hill — The University of North Carolina Press

COPYRIGHT, 1960, BY

THE UNIVERSITY OF NORTH CAROLINA PRESS

The following list shows sources from which pictures were gathered:
Aeck Associates, 75, 132 (bottom)
Alderman, 50 (top), 86, 87, 88, 90, 91
Allied Photographic Illustrators, 64
Architects Collaborative, 82
*Architectural Forum,* 57
*Architectural Record,* 60 (top)
A. L. Aydelott and Associates, 96, 97, 123
J. F. Barnwell, 147
Barron, Heinberg and Brocato, 79 (bottom)
Gabriel Benzur, 65, 74, 122
Blair Collection, 23
Joseph N. Boaz, 45
Eduardo Catalano, 152 (bottom)
J. Wesley Cooper, 20
Curtis and Davis, 37, 99 (top)
Robert Damora, 83
Edwards and Portman, 77
Finch, Alexander, Barnes, Rothchild, and Paschal, 39 (bottom)
James W. Fitzgibbon, 42 (bottom)
Florida Southern College, 58 (bottom), 59 (bottom)
Lionel Freedman, 104
Alexandre Georges, 80 (bottom), 81 (top), 137, 138, 139
Billy Glenn, 42 (top)
Gottscho-Schleisner, 109, 110, 111 (top)
Harmon, Stone, and Keenan, 67
Thomas T. Hayes, Jr., 63
Mrs. Richard Henneman, 13
Philip H. Hiss, 52 (bottom), 53
Holloway, Reeves, and Waugh, 144, 146
André Kertesz, 27
Robert C. Lautman, 28, 29
Lawrence, Saunders, and Calongne, 31
Lisanti, Incorporated, 153, 154, 155, 158, 159, 160, 161
Victor Lundy, 140, 156, 157, 162

Lyles, Bissett, Carlisle, and Wolff, 68 (top), 125, 128
Stuart M. Lynn, 15 (top)
Robert McGinnis, 38, 39 (top)
*Magazine of Building,* 58 (top)
George Matsumoto, 41
Frank L. Miller, 30, 33 (bottom), 34, 36, 46, 47, 60 (bottom), 61, 76, 78, 79 (top), 93, 94, 95, 98, 99 (bottom), 112, 113, 121, 126, 127, 133
Molitor, 33 (top), 40, 48, 49, 62, 68 (bottom), 73, 85, 89, 100, 101, 102, 105 (top), 124, 136
R. M. Morgan, 132 (top), 150, 151
Nashville Housing Authority, 169, 170
Nowicki, Matthew, 105 (bottom)
A. G. Odell, Jr., and Associates, 103
Oliver and Smith, 54, 55, 56
Horace Perry, 80 (top)
Pink, Manning, 84
*Progressive Architecture,* 50 (bottom), 92
Mr. and Mrs. R. T. Reed, 12
Paul Rudolph, 51, 52 (top)
Sherlock, Smith and Adams, 81 (bottom)
Short and Murrell, 35
Small and Boaz, 117, 118
Stevens and Wilkinson, 111 (bottom)
Ezra Stoller, 148, 149
TVA, 163, 164, 165, 166, 167, 168
Robert Thomas, 16
Toombs, Amisano, and Wells, 129, 130, 131
UNC Press, 14
Virginia Museum of Fine Art, 11
Visual Aids, N.C. State College, 152 (top)
Lewis P. Watson, 115, 116, 119, 120, 134, 135
E. W. Waugh, 15 (bottom), 17, 18, 19, 21, 22, 24, 145
Paul Wille, 58 (center), 59 (top and center)
F. Carter Williams, 114

# Preface

THIS BOOK is in no sense an attempt to give a comprehensive survey of southeastern architecture. It does aim to assess what is most characteristic and most striking in modern times and in so doing to examine the genesis of contemporary architecture generally south of the Mason-Dixon line and east of the Mississippi River.

Most tourist outsiders, having been fed on the propaganda of Williamsburg, Tryon's Palace, and the New Orleans French Quarter, have written off the culture of the Southeast as inferior to that of their own provinces. This book, in exploring the renascent building culture of Dixie, shows the error in that dogmatic, uncritical, and undocumented judgment. It is true that Williamsburg should have been copyrighted after the restoration, and no doubt the Rockefellers would have done it after pouring their millions into what they thought would be a national museum, if the restoration's immediate influence could have been accurately foreseen. Williamsburg is now, however, coming into proper focus in the South as an authentic documentation of the South's architectural heritage, and the enlightened Southerner is ready to use the lessons of Williamsburg to continue and build onto the building culture of our time. This book explores that dynamic effort.

The author of this book is Edward W. Waugh, Associate Professor of Architecture in the School of Design at North Carolina State College from 1948 to 1951, from 1951 to 1958 a practicing architect in North Carolina, and since September, 1958, back at his former North Carolina State College position. Edward Waugh has been ably assisted by his wife, Elizabeth, a competent writer in her own right. The authors acknowledge the assistance of my wife, Mabel, for her painstaking research into the contemporary architecture of the Southeast, using her abilities as a former librarian. My position has been one of advisor, critic, and consultant. In looking over their shoulders I have observed an interesting and critical examination develop toward a knowledge and understanding of the architecture of the Southern region.

HENRY L. KAMPHOEFNER, F.A.I.A.
*February 1, 1960*

# *Acknowledgments*

The authors wish to thank Stella Elizabeth Waugh for cheerfully foregoing some of her pleasures while her parents worked on this book.

And kind thanks go to Mabel Kamphoefner for the preparation of our index.

Of course, our gratitude goes to many, many others for assistance of one kind or another, large and small. But particularly we wish to thank John W. Shirley and members of North Carolina State's Faculty Research and Development Fund for financial aid during the period of research; Visual Aids at North Carolina State for photographic assistance; all the architects here represented for time and effort in sending us material; and the photographers who so capably recorded the architects' work.

THE AUTHORS

Raleigh, North Carolina
February 1, 1960

# Table of Contents

| | |
|---|---|
| Preface, by Henry L. Kamphoefner, F.A.I.A. | v |
| Acknowledgments | vi |
| List of Illustrations | viii |
| I. The South and Its Architecture | 3 |
| II. The Contemporary House in the South | 25 |
| III. The Contemporary Southern School | 43 |
| IV. Community and Institutional Buildings | 69 |
| V. Commercial and Industrial Buildings | 106 |
| VI. Trends and Purposes | 141 |
| Index | 171 |

# *Illustrations*

| | |
|---|---:|
| University of Virginia, Charlottesville, Virginia | 11 |
| Edgehill, near Fredericksburg, Virginia | 12 |
| George Edwards residence, Charleston, South Carolina | 13 |
| Map of Savannah in 1757 | 14 |
| Casa Merieult, Royal Street, New Orleans, Louisiana | 15 |
| Twin late nineteenth-century houses, Savannah, Georgia | 15 |
| Slave market, Louisville, Georgia | 16 |
| Town houses, Mobile, Alabama | 17 |
| City market, Charleston, South Carolina | 18 |
| Masonic Temple, Charleston, South Carolina | 19 |
| Bontura, Natchez, Mississippi | 20 |
| A coastal mansion, near Mobile, Alabama | 21 |
| Railroad station, Hogansville, Georgia | 22 |
| Moses Building, Montgomery, Alabama | 23 |
| Cotton Exchange Building, Savannah, Georgia | 24 |
| De Soto Hotel, Savannah, Georgia | 24 |
| Kamphoefner residence, Raleigh, North Carolina | 27 |
| Goodman residence, Alexandria, Virginia | 28-29 |
| Freedman residence, New Orleans, Louisiana | 30-31 |
| Shushan residence, Harahan, Louisiana | 33 |
| Short residence, Baton Rouge, Louisiana | 34-35 |
| Harkey residence, Pascagoula, Mississippi | 36-37 |
| Alexander residence, Atlanta, Georgia | 38-39 |

| | |
|---|---|
| Matsumoto residence, Raleigh, North Carolina | 40-41 |
| Daniel residence, Knoxville, Tennessee | 42 |
| Dormitory, Atlantic Christian College, Wilson, North Carolina | 45 |
| Thomy Lafon School, New Orleans, Louisiana | 46-47 |
| Wilson Junior High School, Mecklenburg County, North Carolina | 48-50 |
| Riverview High School, Sarasota, Florida | 51-53 |
| Princess Anne County High School, Virginia | 54-56 |
| Florida Southern College, Lakeland, Florida | 57-59 |
| Mississippi Hospital School for Cerebral Palsy, Jackson, Mississippi | 60-61 |
| College Union building, North Carolina State College, Raleigh, North Carolina | 62 |
| Married students housing, North Carolina State College, Raleigh, North Carolina | 63 |
| Laboratory and classroom building, Christian Brothers College, Memphis, Tennessee | 64 |
| Dormitory, Oglethorpe University, Atlanta, Georgia | 65 |
| Dormitories, University of South Carolina, Columbia, South Carolina | 66-67 |
| New campus, Clemson College, South Carolina | 68 |
| Coliseum, Georgia Institute of Technology, Atlanta, Georgia | 73 |
| Stadium, Henry Grady High School, Atlanta, Georgia | 74-75 |
| Library, New Orleans, Louisiana | 76 |
| Proposed medical building, Atlanta, Georgia | 77 |
| Library, Natchitoches, Louisiana | 78-79 |
| Harlan Memorial Hospital, Harlan, Kentucky | 80-81 |
| Proposed civic center, Tallahassee, Florida | 82-83 |
| Courthouse, Montgomery, Alabama | 84 |
| Coliseum, Winston-Salem, North Carolina | 85 |
| Civic center, Charlotte, North Carolina | 86-92 |
| Immaculate Conception Church, Marrero, Louisiana | 93-95 |
| Nurses' home and school, Bristol, Tennessee | 96-97 |
| Pediatric clinic, Bayou LaFourche, Louisiana | 98-99 |

| | |
|---|---:|
| Concordia Lutheran Church, Conover, North Carolina | 100-3 |
| Livestock Judging Pavilion, Raleigh, North Carolina | 104-5 |
| Rich's Department Store, Knoxville, Tennessee | 109-11 |
| Carib Building, New Orleans, Louisiana | 112-13 |
| Drive-in branch, First National Bank, Raleigh, North Carolina | 114-16 |
| WRAL-TV buildings, Raleigh, North Carolina | 117-20 |
| America-Fore Insurance Group offices, New Orleans, Louisiana | 121 |
| Cotton gin, Georgia Institute of Genetics, Cartersville, Georgia | 122 |
| Office and apartment building, Memphis, Tennessee | 123 |
| Nuclear reactor exhaust stack, North Carolina State College, Raleigh, North Carolina | 124 |
| Associated Building, Columbia, South Carolina | 125 |
| Sustan Garment Manufacturing Company factory, New Orleans, Louisiana | 126-27 |
| Office building and branch bank, South Carolina National Bank, Columbia, South Carolina | 128 |
| Eastgate Shopping Center, Chattanooga, Tennessee | 129-31 |
| Parking building, Atlanta, Georgia | 132 |
| Motel de Ville, New Orleans, Louisiana | 133 |
| Forest Hills Shopping Center, Garner, North Carolina | 134-35 |
| Sales wing, Gregory-Poole Company, Raleigh, North Carolina | 136 |
| Warm Mineral Springs Inn, Sarasota, Florida | 137-40 |
| Proposed classroom building, North Carolina State College, Raleigh, North Carolina | 144-46 |
| Maintenance building, Union Tank Car Company, Baton Rouge, Louisiana | 147 |
| Offices, Reynolds Metals Company, Richmond, Virginia | 148-49 |
| Dinemountain Restaurant, Georgia | 150-51 |
| Meir residence, Raleigh, North Carolina | 152 |
| Bee Ridge Presbyterian Church, Sarasota, Florida | 153-57 |
| Herron residence, Sarasota, Florida | 158-62 |
| Tennessee Valley Authority | 163-68 |
| Urban redevelopment plan, Nashville, Tennessee | 169-70 |

# THE SOUTH BUILDS

# I. *The South and Its Architecture*

WHAT is the significant architecture that has been created in the Southern region in terms of the new architectural ideas and new technology? Has the cultural heritage had any impact on the nature and form of building in the 1950's? Can we now point to any well-designed *contemporary* structure and say that it has been influenced by the regional styles of Williamsburg, of New Orleans, of Charleston, of Natchez? It is hard, if not impossible, to find any such influence except in the pseudo-neo-Georgian, neo-Charlestonian, neo-Orleansean eclectic buildings. These, of course, have scourged the whole South. They derive from the use of mass-produced, catalogue-numbered cast or wrought ironwork, wood columns, Georgian-type doorways, etc. These catalogue items are superimposed and applied upon houses and buildings as a kind of costume that one might wear to a fancy dress ball. To the sensitive, these attempts at recreating the past generate the same feeling that one might get from looking at a well-known piece of sculpture reproduced in a plastic material and offered for sale in a dime store. It is an architectural charade, a mockery of the vigorousness of our forefathers. It is mass building for the kind of "common man" who might as well have a number rather than a name.

The "common man" approach to architecture, as to other creations such as the automobile or the mass-produced picture reproduction for the wall, results in design clichés which range from "ranch-style Georgian" through "New Orleans French and Spanish" to "California modern"—to the sad copies of Frank Lloyd Wright and Ludwig Mies van der Rohe. All of them, of course, are built from uninspired plans with façades to suit the individual owner, who may either have a nostalgic feeling in one of the directions above or be driven by that amorphous and unpredictable force known as public opinion.

The neighborhoods of these new houses and buildings are designed without benefit of any philosophy of organic architecture. Subdivision groupings of them are beginning to choke the approaches to every medium and large city of the South. The sameness which is apparent from Washington to New Orleans, from Richmond to Memphis, is a staggering comment on the aesthetic degradation of a great people. This is clearly and indelibly stamped on one's mind as one drives through the outskirts of the old sections of almost any Southern city. Leaving the few spared trees of the old part and the gracious original houses, one transfers to one of the new subdivisions and sees only the denuded landscape covered with the kinds of houses and buildings just described.

To serve these new dormitory areas of the expanding cities the automobile age has spawned a new kind of shopping center. These centers, too, can be seen everywhere in the South—across the whole United States, in fact. They are built in the center of a sea of asphalt designed to squeeze out the last square foot and square inch of parking space. The bulldozer has run uncontrolled in smashing trees which may have taken a hundred years or more to grow. And nothing in the center's design suggests that there is ever to be replacement of any planting whatsoever.

What has happened to the town pride of the Southerner? What has happened to his architectural sense and feeling for landscape? For while it is true that contemporary architectural design owes little or nothing to the Southern regional architectural traditions, it is also true that Southerners in the past have shown, in terms of their own times, extraordinary flair for the organic approach to architecture that is the essence of the contemporary style. It is not the purpose of this introduction to provide a history of architecture in the South but simply to point to a few highlights in that history which illustrate this point.

The Englishmen who settled Jamestown and Charleston and Savannah, and the French and Spanish who settled St. Augustine and Mobile and

New Orleans, did not come to the New World to establish a new architecture. They brought with them their native crafts and traditional ideas of building houses. The first houses they built, after they were sufficiently settled to think of more than basic shelter, were houses they might have built in their native lands. The English settlers undoubtedly had with them the construction handbooks prepared by the carpenter guilds for master carpenters to follow. And later, in the eighteenth century, they had such elaborate architectural style books as Salmon's *Palladio Londinensis,* Gibbs's *Book of Architecture,* Adam's *Vitruvius Scoticus,* and Leoni's *Designs of A. Palladio,* which made available to them the plans and details of the best Renaissance architects of England and the Continent.

But New World conditions immediately offered challenges and opportunities, and American building began to take on a character of its own as the colonists made the most of the new environment. First of all was the change in building material. In contrast to Europe's shrinking forests and scarce timber, the new country offered a superabundance of wood—in fact, forests had to be destroyed to make cultivation possible. What was more natural than to substitute for the brick wall of the English Renaissance house the wood frame wall of the American colonial house? Later, disastrous fires dictated the use of brick and plaster construction, especially for urban houses and public buildings of a permanent character. Many of the plantation homes of the very wealthy were also of solid brick or stone masonry. But for the most part the new country became a land of wooden houses.

Among the colonies, Virginia made perhaps fewer modifications than any of the others in the traditional style of English architecture. For a number of reasons, Virginia did not develop towns during the colonial period, and the country houses of the tobacco planters set the style of the colony—a style which strongly influenced all the rest of the South. The use of the center hall and the building of houses one room deep may be taken as evidence of adaptation to the hot summer climate, but it must be said that, on the whole, Virginia did not contribute much in the way of new forms and ideas to the Georgian architecture of England except to adapt it to the use of wood construction. Speaking generally, it was not until the first quarter of the nineteenth century that Virginia began to lose its awe of the Georgian sufficiently to add porches to the front and rear for the purpose of outdoor living during the hot summers. It is nevertheless true that Virginia Georgian, with that of South Carolina, set the standard of "quality" for 150 years for those parts of the South not affected by French and Spanish influences. And it is also true that architecturally the most enduring group of buildings designed in the South up to now is the Jeffersonian complex at the University of Virginia. Here is a great and simple idea for higher education expressed with brilliant clarity and skill, unparalleled in any similar cohesive group of college buildings in the Western world.

South of Virginia, a true urban culture with a distinctive architecture sprang up in Charleston. Founded in 1670 by the British in one of the best natural harbors on the eastern coast, Charleston became, with Boston, New York, Philadelphia, and Baltimore, one of the leading colonial port cities. Coastal trading kept it in close touch with these other cities, as well as with the British, French, and Spanish cities of the West Indies, the Caribbean, and the Gulf of Mexico. Though predominantly English, the colony was stimulated by the influx of Huguenots, who brought with them their trades and crafts and architectural inclinations. The first Huguenot church founded in America and other public buildings still standing in Charleston proclaim this influence. It is likely that some of the early wrought iron forms which were used structurally as well as decoratively in the Charleston town houses came directly from Huguenot craftsmen.

Charleston's major contribution to American architecture was in the development of the town house. While the planters of Virginia tended to stay on their plantations the year round, coming to the capital at Williamsburg only for brief visits, the South Carolina rice and indigo planters made Charleston their home for large parts of the year, building permanent town houses for themselves. The rural architecture of South Carolina does not differ greatly from that of Virginia, but the famous Charleston town-house type, with its two-story side verandah overlooking its private garden, remains one of the finest examples in this country of architecture organically adapted to its environment.

Charleston had been an established city with a fine architectural tradition for sixty years when Oglethorpe founded the city of Savannah, a hundred miles away, in 1733. Savannah is almost unique in the fact that the settlers left England with a beautifully conceived plan for their city, which they proceeded to execute. However, on reflection it is not surprising that people setting out to build a new city in the late Renaissance period of English architecture should feel the need for a city plan. One of the greatest contributions of the late Renaissance architects in England and in France is the development of the architectural city plan. The magnificent crescent in the city of Bath, England, the Adelphi Terrace in London, the development of Lincoln's Inn, the beautiful Georgian squares of Kensington, can be said to have found parallel expression in Savannah, perhaps unequalled and certainly unlike any other city of the South.

Here is a city with a well-designed waterfront that is practical for shipping on the river side and on the street side faces a well-planted and well-shaded boulevard. It is a city bounded by tree-lined boulevards and interspersed every two blocks in either direction by grand planted squares. It is all as purposeful and useful and inviting today as it ever was. Savannah houses and the buildings around the planted squares show that their designers had a consciousness of the architectural environment of which they were a part. Here, in essence, is magnificent aesthetic discipline expressed in a city complex with a broad and uncluttered architectural imagination.

While Charleston was characterized by the side verandah with the walled street-door entrance, Savannah favored front entrances and side and rear porches. This characteristic is peculiar not only to Georgian houses of the city but also to the mid- and late-Victorian Savannah town house. The beautiful planted boulevards of Savannah undoubtedly made their aesthetic impact on the later towns of Georgia, for one of the features apparent in nearly all of the smaller mid-Georgian towns is the magnificent avenues of still unviolated shade trees.

New Orleans is still another world. It too is a city of great architectural heritage. Its taste and architectural expression dominated the whole lower Mississippi Valley and the Gulf Coast for a century. Here the cultures of Spain and France fused to produce a subtropical colonial city of great wealth and architectural taste. Both had a Mediterranean architectural tradition which had developed from the thrust of the Italian Renaissance on these countries and had matured with due regard for the regional needs of the mild Mediterranean climate. It is not unnatural therefore that New Orleans in its Vieux Carré should have grown into a city of houses and shops adapted to hot weather, since it came so directly from southern European shores. Spain and southern France already had a tradition of ironwork grills used in the baroque manner.

The basis of the ironwork of New Orleans houses was the need to have balconies which would serve as places for sitting outdoors on warm days and nights and also would shield windows from the sun. Early wrought and later cast iron columns with stiffening brackets, and screens, gates, fences, and balconies, were an extremely logical use of iron. Patterns developed which at first sight seem entirely ornamental but which on closer study are invariably functional, although they make superb use of symbolic forms.

The New Orleans solution to the town house is the two-story dwelling with its street façade pierced by a carriageway leading to a rear courtyard. The courtyard separates the house from the slave quarters, and side walls protect the private patio from the neighboring houses. Here is one of the great architectural contributions to town-house living. Contemporary architecture might well scrutinize the principles expressed in these houses to see whether something has not been lost in designing modern town houses on narrow and restricted city lots with no thought to outdoor privacy.

In the early days of the American republic (New Orleans and the Louisiana Territory became a part of it in 1804), there was a merging of regional architectural idioms in what has been called the Federal style. But this was not at the expense of all regional variations: for example, the town houses of Charleston and Savannah achieved their finest and most distinctive forms in the nineteenth century. And in the lower Mississippi Valley there developed an architecture indigenous to the region, though its European origins remained evident. It took root and grew, acquiring new characteristics in the dense, misty bayou country and along the magnificent shore line of the Gulf.

The national styles of the first half of the nineteenth century—Greek Revival, Gothic Revival, and all the other manifestations of romanticism—had their vogue in the South as in the rest of the nation, but their progress was rudely arrested by the cataclysm of Civil War and its resulting improvishment of the entire region for two or three generations. Southern industrialism had only begun to grow in the decade before the War. There were few cities of any size—Richmond, Charleston, Memphis, New Orleans. It is symptomatic for the entire region that in Charleston there is practically no evidence in the old city of any significant building after 1865.

But by the end of the century a new South was definitely on the way, no less in architecture than in a revived agriculture and a new industry. No more vital example of the thrust and drive of the tardily arriving industrial revolution can be found than the late-Victorian De Soto Hotel in Savannah. This building makes one pause and ask whether here is not the essence of the architectural spirit which directed Richardson, Sullivan, and Wright along a course that was to be followed by many for the next sixty years. Perhaps these three are to be considered the last of the great Victorians rather than the first of the twentieth-century architects. In any case, the South is rich in the tradition of a vital architecture of the late industrial revolution. Perhaps this architecture marks the end of an era of great steamboats, cotton exchanges, market places, railroad stations.

Today, in the middle of the twentieth century, we can look back more objectively and more appreciatively at the architecture of the late-Victorian period which is so well illustrated in parts of the South. Here was an architecture of the self-made man, of the industrialist who rose from factory hand to president of the company. It came from the age of steam machines but it never forgot that people made the steam engine, and so it was a human architecture, completely unself-conscious and eclectic. It could borrow at will a bit from Egyptian, Romanesque, Gothic, all periods of the Renaissance, and throw in some of the designer's own creativity, to produce an essentially humanistic piece of work.

By 1920 the age of technology had begun to have its effect on the cultural expression of the whole South. The statistician and the efficiency expert moved into solid positions in the growing industrial empires. People were now described in terms of "per capita" and "needs per annum" and no longer as flesh and blood. The production line and the distribution system for the line became the means and end for the new factories. This kind of cultural climate had no place for any aesthetic tradition. The fine early town planning ideas, for instance, which were introduced and so carefully planted by Oglethorpe and his colony at Savannah were completly lost to the efficiency experts who set up business all over the South—and the nation. All the mistakes in the black country of England—Birmingham and Coventry—and in this country—Pittsburgh, Philadelphia, Cleveland—were being repeated with the congested slum-breeding cities, the tightly compacted houses around an odorous and smoke-producing factory core where land was treated as a commodity so precious that not an extra square foot could be devoted to parks, playground, green belts. And it must be said here that these mistakes, on a much larger scale, are still being made.

The Southern region at the time of the 1929 stock crash had just recovered from the devastation of the post-bellum period and its larger cities were being swamped by the mediocrity and vulgarity beginning to be accepted as "achievement" by Madison Avenue. The depression of the 1930's came to the emerging South as the final shock in a series that began in 1861. Capital improvement ground to a stop. The successive Roosevelt administrations put government into the business of rescuing jobless craftsmen and artists. In the South as well as in the rest of the nation, federal, county, and city buildings were built with government aid in order to prime the pumps of the construction industry. Whatever the economic effect, architecture suffered from a sterile, bureaucratic control which stifled the imagination and initiative of the creative architect.

Architecture in the Southern region in the 1930's approached as near to the doldrums as it could without disappearing completely as a social art. The architect, a vigorous and flourishing influence in late nineteenth-century culture, had by now lost his position as a leader. The engineer was rapidly replacing the architect in many areas because the engineer's training peculiarly suited him to fit into an age that operated in terms of statistical analysis without regard for other values. And by the end of the 1930's the architect, once, like Wren, a structural designer, had deteriorated into a mere decorator of façades. The professional schools played their part in training this kind of architect by turning to Paris as the fountainhead of all architectural thought and slavishly imitating the ideas of the Beaux Arts school. While the Beaux Arts schools were turning out the decorator-type architect, there were other schools in the South, such as Georgia Tech and North Carolina State College, which leaned heavily toward the architectural-engineering approach to training. This tended to emphasize elements of building construction at the expense of integrated, organic design. And it might be said that the architects practicing in the South in the late 1930's can be classified loosely into either the building-decorator type or the architectural-engineering type.

To tell the story of the effects of World War II and its aftermath on Southern—and American—architecture, it is necessary to go back to the early days of the century. As already mentioned, Frank Lloyd Wright's place in architecture can perhaps be best understood if he is thought of not as the first of the modern architects but as the last of the great Victorians. Philip Johnson has called Wright the greatest architect of the nineteenth century. To have said these things even ten years ago would have been considered architectural heresy coming from any architect carrying the torch for the new architecture. But now we can look back more objectively on the past which generated the architecture of Wright. Perhaps the major difference between him and his Victorian contemporaries is that he departed entirely from the eclectic borrowing used by the Victorians, even though he began by using the heavy masonry which the Victorians loved so much, the brick arches, the wide overhang, and the simple hipped roof of the country railroad station.

When one traces the source of the emergence of the new architecture in the South, Wright is important because he stood almost alone in the Western world against the decadent creations of the period from 1900 through the 1930's. It was not in this country that he made his first significant impact but in Holland, where men like Dudok, Wijdeveld, and Oud welcomed him with open arms. The most important contribution that he made to the continuance of architecture as a great art form was to take the "form follows function" premise of his early teacher, Louis Sullivan, and of those before Sullivan and to restate it consciously and vigorously in organic building. Wright was a prolific writer and publicist as well as designer. His precepts of organic architecture were like a new battle cry to the few sensitive practitioners left in Europe who were willing to risk commercial success in order to keep architecture alive. The struggle went on from the early part of the century through the depression years, but few in America took up the cause at that time.

In Germany in the early part of the century another group of architects was searching for new forms with which to express the twentieth century. Called the Bauhaus school, their most important members were Walter Gropius and his colleague, Ludwig Mies van der Rohe. These men were undoubtedly influenced in their early years by Wright. In France the Swiss expatriate, Le Corbusier, began to have an impact, as the elder Saarinen and Alva Aalto did in Scandinavia. It was not long before it became apparent that these men were proceeding on a line of development of their own devising. They believed in the ordered modular sequence of the new production-line factory. Rolled-steel beams and columns could now be made with precision and in great quantities. Glass could be poured in large sheets, and shallow steel beams could span wide spaces. They emphasized the integrity of architectural expression with the materials. The result might be described as a formal architecture, particularly the work of Mies van der Rohe. The structure or the skeleton now became the motivating element of building design, and in the case of steel, careful statistical analysis determined the ideal spacing of columns to give the most economical beam sizes.

Just as Palladio dominated the architecture of the late Italian Renaissance, the order of Mies van der Rohe has come to dominate the architecture of today. His aesthetics is the aesthetics of fine art, just as the aesthetics of the Parthenon was the culmination of fine art expression of early Greece. In a sense Mies van der Rohe's architecture is the refined architecture of the intellectual rather than the architecture of human drive and emotion. It is an architecture of the white corpuscles rather than the red. Here, then, in Mies van der Rohe and Wright we have the two extremes which are generating the significant new architectural forms not only in the South but in the Western world generally. Perhaps the true architecture which our culture is seeking lies somewhere between the formalism of Mies van der Rohe and the humanism of Wright.

The nature of architecture makes it a peculiarly complex and difficult profession to pursue. Perhaps this complexity is even truer in the middle of the twentieth century than it was a hundred years ago. It is certainly truer than it was two hundred years ago. Even so, in all ages, good architecture has been achieved only by a true rapport between architect and client. The architect can operate only within the sphere of his client's understanding, economic means, and aesthetic sensibilities. The designer in the South today is often faced with the problem of convincing a timid client that the architectural heritage of the South is no longer a copyable idiom. In addition to these difficulties, he is faced with the job of accommodating the modern building to the specialized system of wires, ducts, pipes, and equipment which are necessary for the artificial human environment we demand today. A modern hotel, for example, is no longer just a piece of architecture, as earlier practitioners conceived it. It has become as complex a piece of machinery as an ocean-going liner. A full realization of this change has come upon the architect only within the last twenty or thirty years.

The rapid change in the approach to architectural practice along with the complete revolution in architectural philosophy has been far beyond the capacity of the average "businessman" architect. He has often been bewildered and confused and has taken the easiest course, which has been to provide a kind of automatic design-draftsman service for the whims of the uninformed client. It is a good thing that after World War II there were still many influential and informed architects and people who had achieved a full enough understanding of the meaning of their evolving society to know that architecture had to be revived if fullness of living were to prevail over mediocrity. The action taken by these people, once the way was clear, has resulted in the renascence of the architectural schools of the South, which had, in most cases, deteriorated into draftsman-training schools. Cases in point are the revitalization of architectural teaching in North Carolina State College, Georgia Tech, and Tulane and the recent creation of a school of architecture under its own dean at Clemson. All of these schools and others in the South are dedicated to the new architecture. They are served by faculties with integrity and strong enough convictions to imbue their students with the meaning of the architecture of the twentieth century. These schools, some of which have been in operation on the new basis from ten to twelve years, are already providing leading architects for better planning and building in the South.

In spite of the Southern mistakes and apathy which have been criticized in earlier pages, the new approach to architecture has become a reality in many cities and small towns of the South. One of the significant building forms which has been almost universally accepted is the contemporary public school. Part of the credit for the adoption of better designs in these public buildings must go to North Carolina, where legislative foresight prepared the way in 1949 for a $50,000,000 state bond issue which swelled to $125,000,000 when the local bonds of the cities, counties, and towns were added. The North Carolina State Board of Education and the Superintendent of Public Instruction made it clear to the architects and the school boards that they felt that the schoolhouses built during the depression years under PWA and the schoolhouses of the 1920's were not the buildings to serve a modern educational system in a progressive state.

To this end they called for the advice and counsel of the faculty of the newly formed School of Design in Raleigh to help develop design criteria for schools and to help convince the school boards and some of the practicing architects that the time had come for a new approach. The result was an almost total adoption of contemporary design for school buildings in the state. The movement spread rapidly to other Southern states during the 1950's.

Comparing the new schools of the South with those of other states (California, for instance, which at this time claims to have the most progressive school plants in the world) makes it evident that the leading architects of the South have earned their places among the best. Naturally, while most schools in the South today are "modern," not all of them are good. Sometimes architectural contracts are awarded on the basis of political influence rather than ability. Nevertheless, for the most part, the results achieved in school design show that there is opportunity for the good architect-client team to produce fine institutional buildings anywhere in the South today.

As for expanding college campuses and buildings, the case of North Carolina presents interesting contrasts. In 1958 both the Presbyterians and the

Methodists decided independently to found and underwrite new liberal arts colleges in the state. In both instances the building committees carefully selected their architects on the basis of recognized and outstanding ability. And yet, while these denominations have shown such an enlightened approach to their campus design problems, only a short ten years earlier the people sponsoring the resettlement of Wake Forest College in Winston-Salem, with a clean piece of ground to start with, missed a unique opportunity to give the South a magnificent contemporary university campus. Instead, they were responsible for a group of buildings whose exteriors represent the absolute in nostalgic pseudo-neo-Georgian without a modicum of twentieth-century expression except for the asphalted parking lots. However, some attempt has been made to bring the interiors into line with the most conservative in modern design practice—an expensive architectural masquerade.

In the translation of the needs of our teeming universities into architectural form it may be said that the South, although in some cases it could be accused of looking backward to traditional architecture, is in the forefront of the nation in its openness to new ideas. There is a growing demand for integrated, long-range architectural planning in dozens of Southern universities.

The techniques of construction in the last twenty years, particularly in the South, where methods have been more archaic than in the rest of the country, have changed rapidly from the handcraft approach to a thoroughgoing machine technology. Buildings are now conceived as consisting of ready-made components taken from the stock inventory of the producer and integrated into the building. Where it is not possible to use premanufactured items, diverse kinds of machinery have been developed, from the portable electric saw to the ready-mix concrete plant, to eliminate or speed up on-the-site labor. Local plants make up special items of metal, wood, etc., in their shops. Complete buildings, even small houses, do not lend themselves to production-line techniques for the simple reason that a house is too bulky to ship unless it is broken down into relatively small parts. While there are many prefabricated houses available, they have been too rigid in their designs to have had great appeal.

Although a great deal of individual work is still performed by building mechanics at the site of the building, this is becoming less and less the case except for the assembling of components shipped in by the manufacturer. The use of metals in large buildings is gaining at a tremendous pace, because they can be adapted to all types of manufacturing methods. While steel still predominates as the structural skeleton for most large buildings because of its adaptability to being rolled, shaped, punched, and connected, reinforced concrete is being accepted in the South as a competitor. One major reason for this is that fire regulations require that the steel framework of large buildings be covered with two-inch concrete to stop twisting and buckling under extreme heat. Prefabricated and prestressed concrete components are also being used, as well as tilt-up concrete walls and tilt-up structural frames. The concrete lift slab is another labor-saving device coming into wide use.

If concrete structures continue to gain in popularity, this will bring back more on-the-site labor than is generally used at present. The great drawback of concrete, however, is its excessive weight. It is probable that the use of concrete will not realize the full promise that it shows at present except in areas where stone, sand, and cement are close at hand.

The urbanization of the South under the impact of industrialization is the central, dominant factor in its present situation. Yet it is all too plain that the profession of architecture has failed in the South to foresee, to plan, and to recognize the city and town as a complex of buildings which constitute an architectural environment. Architects as a group have become preoccupied with the design of individual buildings and the kind of credit this brings them. They have left the growing and sprawling Southern city to be taken care of by the speculator, the traffic statistician, the sanitary engineer, and the highway engineer—or any other practitioner carrying the title of "specialist" or "planner."

As a result, the Southern city is growing today like a cancer rather than a healthy tissue. Each new individual or commercial enterprise that the city manages to capture generates in the suburbs more low-standard housing approved by the FHA as being adequate for American families. Streets that should be quiet are given over entirely to automobiles. There is no provision for children or their mothers to walk to school. Super-expressways slice through areas indiscriminately, amputating whole neighborhoods and destroying all possibility of developing any master plan. The domination of the automobile extends everywhere, from factory, department store, and shopping center to school, church, and home. In his rush to industrialize and urbanize, the Southerner has forgotten his tradition of gracious living.

While architects as a group have not provided the leadership that they might have, there are architects in the South who have the imagination and the training needed to give Southern cities the best standard of good living yet attained. This would mean an environment in which the automobile again became the servant of man, in which schools and churches would again be accessible by foot, in which permanent green-belt protection extended around residential areas. But the achievement of such an environment will require action by the Southern people, for it can be obtained only if Southerners voluntarily limit the populations of their growing towns and cities by statewide and inter-regional planning, so that when one city has reached its optimum, another small town may be selected to become the next small city. The optimum population of a town that is good to live in is probably about sixty thousand, divided into five or six neighborhoods of about ten thousand, each with its individual elementary school and shopping center and a common central shopping center and high school.

The South prides itself as being the home of American democracy, the home of Washington and Jefferson. Perhaps it can take new democratic action to achieve and perpetuate a better way of living. The challenge is here, now, and awaits the demand of the public for the kind of environment that the better architect-planners are trained to provide. Most people seem unaware that this can be done at less cost to the individual taxpayer than his present "stop-gap" planning system is costing him. It is the duty of the architect, if he calls himself a professional man, to support vigorously a program which will save the towns and cities of this magnificent region from the calamity that will inevitably result from lack of planning, overgrowth, and decay.

The original University of Virginia buildings at Charlottesville, Virginia, were designed by Thomas Jefferson around 1819. The photograph here is a view looking up the mall (called the Lawn) toward the Rotunda building. Jefferson's design is probably unique as a solution for a university campus because of its extreme flexibility and the integrated order which it creates. This can be seen in the series of two-story buildings which face each other across the Lawn and are connected by one-story colonnaded rows of students' rooms. The buildings have upper-floor balconies so that the lower floors become a continuation of the colonnade connection. In the Jeffersonian plan each of these two-storied buildings housed a professor with his family, with classrooms on the first floor. These houses, on the sides facing away from the Lawn, had serpentine walls enclosing private gardens, which are well known. Deliveries to the houses, coach service, and the like were brought in between these walled gardens which left one end of the Lawn open and free. It is too bad that Jefferson's concept was not maintained and that a neo-classical group of buildings has since shut off the openness. It can readily be seen that this plan adapts itself uniquely to the contemporary university campus with its automobile problems. A series of malls such as this could be placed between a series of dead-end service drives from the fronting main road, and the open ends of these malls could be pedestrian ways.

Edgehill, near Fredericksburg, Virginia, while it is not one of the much publicized mansions of early Virginia, is perhaps more typical of the average plantation architecture of the period. The house is pure English Georgian in its fenestration, its use of brick, and in the simple detailing of its interior. The original plan consisted of an entrance hall passing through the house, with the great room on the left, a semi-basement below, and a large dormitory room at the gable end above. An addition to the main block of the house on the right made the plan symmetrical and produced the well-known center-hall colonial type. The house is superbly sited on a high knoll, and all of the original rooms have windows on two façades. The spacious hall acts like a Venturi tube, and even today is a choice spot for the owners to find a breeze on a summer night. The evolution of a Southern country house can be detected in the façade. The late Victorian owners placed a front porch across the main entrance and its two flanking windows. In the twentieth-century restoration the owners regarded only the original form as valid and removed the porch.

The George Edwards house in Charleston is a fine example of the so-called "single house" style of town residence. This type is prevailingly rectangular in plan, with the short side on the street and the long side facing the garden. Note that the end of the lower porch on the street side has been enclosed, with an entrance doorway of great richness, providing privacy along with exposure to the summer breezes.

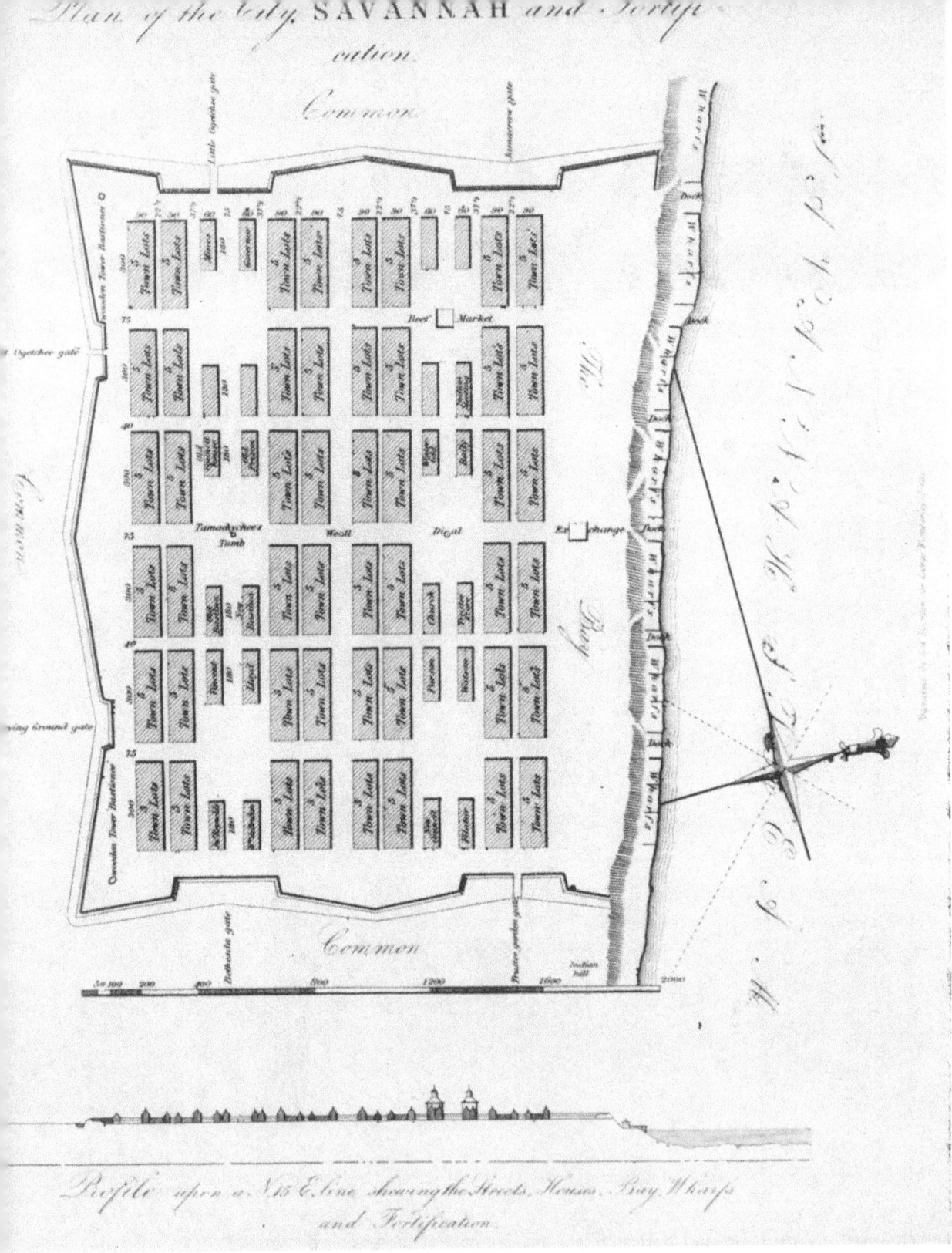

This map of Savannah in 1757 (from Nichols and Johnston, *The Early Architecture of Georgia*) shows all the features of its unique plan, many of which survive to this day. The last of the British colonies to be founded, Georgia was from the start the product of a highly conscious colonizing effort. It had more carefully planned towns than any of the other colonies, and interesting plans survive of such towns as Macon, Augusta, Milledgeville, Columbus, and Brunswick.

Casa Merieult on Royal Street was built in 1792 and it is an excellent example of an original New Orleans patio house. It demonstrates the use of the upper-floor cantilevered balcony as a means of communication, as a sun and breeze control device, and as a platform for reaching the louvred shutters when they are fastened open. An outdoor garden, easy to maintain and completely private from the street, is an important contribution made to architecture by this type of house.

These twin late-nineteenth-century Savannah town houses with their simple Georgian-type façades bear eloquent testimony to the taste of their original owner and architect. The entrance leading from above the English basement is characteristic of these Savannah speculation houses of the period.

15

Slave Market, Louisville, Georgia, built in 1758. This building is a prime example of a simple, straightforward approach to post- and beam-construction. It uses diagonal brackets at the top of the post for bracing, and a plain hipped roof made of heavy timber framing and sheathed with hand-split wood shingles. If the cupola were left off, the building would achieve a quiet dignity worthy of the best twentieth-century contemporary architect. However, the cupola was then important to the city's life in that it housed an imported warning bell for emergencies.

The Mediterranean influence upon this group of town houses in Mobile, Alabama, makes one wonder if the group is located in the United States or on the shores of southern France. The long French windows with the louvred shutters and the balcony with the fine wrought iron balustrade supported by the curled brackets further identify the influence of its origin.

A town house in Mobile, Alabama. The wrought iron of Charleston and New Orleans gave way to cast iron in the mid-nineteenth century, and in some cases the later forms of the cast iron exceeded in beauty the earlier wrought iron. This house is a fine example of the delicacy which the cast iron craftsmen achieved, particularly the fine tracery of the porch roof. The columns could have been so slender only in a material such as iron, and the curved steps with their pierced risers and treads and their spidery balustrade show to what extent delicate members can attain adequate strength when a material such as cast iron is handled by a competent designer and produced by an excellent craftsman. New Orleans firms' imprints have been found on much cast iron used in the South, but much of it was imported from Philadelphia.

The Charleston city market was the hub of economic life and is a masterful piece of civic planning. It has an imposing classical office building on Meeting Street and is situated as if it were a locomotive leading a string of flat cars, the flat cars being a series of market halls strung out in an easterly direction for several blocks behind the building toward the busy docks on the Cooper River. On either side are streets which enable the farmers to bring their produce in on one side and the buyers to cart their purchases out on the other. While the building was designed for horsedrawn vehicles, it works today equally well for the automobile. The interior is one of the market halls behind the main offices. The designer of the halls could have been the best of contemporary architects. He analyzed his architectural problem with magnificent clarity and solved it with brilliant simplicity, as can be seen, by the use of equally spaced brick columns supporting simple, flat A-frame roof trusses to span the hall. The spaces between the columns are wide enough for farm wagons to back up to and disgorge their contents onto the tables. Using the arched openings at the ends of each hall, the buyers could move axially from the front end of the market at the west all the way through the series of halls to the east. Not only did the architect solve the major traffic and circulation problems in a planning way but he used the problem to develop the structural theme of each of the market halls and introduced, at the upper level of the openings between the masonry columns, wood louvres to control the sun and ventilation.

Even the better contemporary architects occasionally overlook the importance of designing carefully every single element and component of a building. This was not true generally in the nineteenth century when, except for the commercial false fronts, buildings were designed in great detail. Here, for example, is the fire escape at the back of the Masonic Temple at Charleston. It is a brilliant piece of pure design expertly executed by wrought iron craftsmen with outstanding ability. This same stairway could do justice to any good contemporary building. It is free of the wall and is supported by wrought iron brackets which cantilever out from the masonry wall under the landings.

Bontura, the Natchez, Mississippi, house shown here, is architecture in evolution. Built on the Natchez bluff before 1790, it has undergone the various occupations of Spanish, French, and English and was damaged in the Civil War. Nevertheless, no architectural detail has been added that mars its total effect. It is still an elegant town house which shows the influence of climate and merging cultures, and the effectiveness of New Orleans ironwork.

A coastal mansion near Mobile, Alabama. This house faces the Gulf Coast and was built by A. Samuels in 1873. The screened porch was originally an open gallery. While this house uses the elements of the Greek Revival with its Corinthian colonnaded gallery, there is no question that it is a Victorian house, because it shows a whimsical lightness of touch and a refusal to be enslaved by Palladian dogma. The entablature is deep, and a rhythm, picked up from the colonnade, is introduced into the small repetitive obligato of the consoles. Such license is what adds the charm to this kind of Victorian architecture. Even the screening of the gallery has been delicately carried out and adds to the over-all cohesiveness. Houses all along the Gulf Coast are of every kind and description, and one can follow the whole history of Southern residential architectural trends perhaps better here, driving along the coast proper, than anywhere else in the South. Regardless of the contemporary blight of hot dog stands, motels, and amusement spots on the nearby beaches, these Gulf Coast houses cannot be matched anywhere along any other coast for originality, use of surrounding trees, and variation.

This Hogansville, Georgia, railroad station was built circa 1916; but it is typical of such buildings built all over the South in the late nineteenth and early twentieth centuries. This building type is constructed with heavy brick masonry bearing walls and a hipped roof with tremendous shadowy overhangs to protect the passengers on both the street and rail sides from rain or hot sun. A study of the architectural form of these village railroad stations shows how closely allied they are to the forms and the use of materials in the early prairie houses of Frank Lloyd Wright.

The Moses Building, built between 1886 and 1888 in Montgomery, Alabama. It was torn down in 1907. It is evidence that Southern architects of the Victorian period had a strong feeling for expressing the iron frame skeleton. If the top floor with its dormer windows and its tower were removed from this building, the viewer would see that it might be a contender for the structural expressionism attributed to Louis Sullivan.

The Cotton Exchange Building, Savannah, Georgia, was completed in 1887. It was designed by William Gibbons Preston, who was the winner of a national competition to select the designer. The building is unusual because it sits on the edge of the steep Savannah River bluff and straddles the street which was platted on Oglethorpe's city plan as running down to the river's edge. The architect solved the problem presented by the location by cutting out a large areaway in front of the building and introducing a series of public stairways for pedestrians and cobblestone ramps for lowering cotton down from the top of the bluff. The cobblestones are as well placed today as ever. The building is typical of the overdecorated late Victorian period when the popular terra cotta column capitals and low frieze sculpture and pediment ornament were freely used. A significant structural feature of the building is the rear wall facing the Savannah River, several stories in height, which is carried on a tremendous composite cast iron main beam.

The De Soto Hotel in Savannah, Georgia, was opened in 1890 with nineteen bathrooms for the original three hundred guest rooms. This building, although its period is late Victorian, does not suffer from the prevalent diseases of that period but shows a vivid and bold approach in its design forms. The use of brick arched masonry openings on a cylindrical drum over a low pantile cantilevered canopy creates a design tour de force which is new and original. When one considers that Richardson, Sullivan, and Wright were only emerging at this time, it is easy to see that this building is in the vanguard of its period.

## II. *The Contemporary House in the South*

SOME few Southerners in the 1940's began to demand dwelling houses which would express the contemporary idiom of the awakening, mid-century South. It was in this area of building that the South saw the first reaction against the architectural nostalgia of the rampant Georgian eclecticism. Many of the original advocates came from the faculties of the architectural schools in the region, and the range of response varied from a formal discipline to a free, almost rural American approach tempered by a new aesthetic.

This divergence developed in the 1940's and it was continuing unabated in the late 1950's. Modern houses can now be classified as the products of three schools of architectural philosophy, two of which can be called "formalist." The first of these is composed of the adherents of strict modular design suggested by steel column and beam framing and interpreted through industrial component parts or by the use of the four-by-eight plywood module and the four-foot prefabricated window. The other group of formalists has developed the architecture of the dwelling as a warped surface or folded-plate space sculpture in which the occupants become consciously and constantly enfolded within its space definition.

The third group, which might be considered the architectural deviant, follows strictly the belief that form must be generated by functional need and that it is therefore impossible to apply a predetermined formalized discipline to any architectural problem. This group is beginning to be known as humanist, although the exponents of the other two philosophies are inclined to call it romantic. The ultimate judge is the discerning member of the Southern public. In the meantime it is healthy for contemporary architecture that three divergent points of view do exist and oppose one another.

In the modern South the need for housing lies in five main areas of development: the town house, the apartment, the low-cost housing development, the suburban house, the town-country exurban house. Whether a house be in the town or outside of it and whether it be formally or informally contemporary, there are certain design principles whose violation brands the house as ill-conceived no matter how good the workmanship. First, a good house must have privacy from its neighbors. This can be achieved on the small urban lot by the use of walls, heavy planting, and proper orientation and placement of the house so that it opens onto its own private garden area. On the larger exurban site it is possible to have a house opened up by glass in all directions if adequate green-belt protection is under the control of its owner. The low-cost house can achieve this kind of privacy too, even though for economy's sake each house may be one of a group of several included in one row or in one building. And, a well-designed apartment can be so oriented that its windows are not overlooked in any way by either the public without or by adjoining neighbors. Furthermore, good soundproofing techniques can isolate each apartment unit acoustically.

Along with the need for privacy goes the need for zoning between the elements of the house itself. Modern living standards require a private area for each member of the family, for reading, studying, and sleeping. At the same time, a common family area is an important element, as is an area in which to entertain friends. Keeping all three of these areas adequately functioning is the task of the utility operation of the house—food preparation, bathroom facilities, and laundry.

The next important requirement of the design of a more livable and better-looking house is the need to fit the house into its topographical environment with due regard for views but without sacrificing the best orientation for the climate. Without a doubt, houses in the South ideally should have all rooms oriented in a southern direction with adequate overhang to cut out the summer sun. Similarly, the house—and bedrooms in particular—should open when possible to the prevailing breezes. If the prevailing winds come from the west, louvres and similar devices may be used. The so-called solar house is a modern term but not a new idea. Vitruvius, writing centuries ago, spoke convincingly of the need to accommodate building design to the characteristics of the sun.

If the architect knows the principles of physics he will also know that white marble chipped roofs reflect the heat-producing infrared rays; that through-ventilated, sloped roofs generate convection air currents to cool the roof space; that rigid insulation placed in contact with the roof surface will develop a radiant heat blanket above the occupants during the early evening hours to the point where the house will be insufferably hot. And even when the house is air-conditioned, the cost of cooling will be excessive.

While the modern architect of the humanist group is in the minority, he has the greater freedom and the greater capacity for making the physical forces of nature work in his favor. The sculptural formalist is defeated at the start if, in his effort to preserve the inherent beauty of the form, he disregards the need for such things as air spaces to cool the roof and ceiling-height partitions to secure acoustical privacy.

As an addendum it must be stated again that all good architects, particularly in the expanding South, go beyond the problems of house design and advise their clients on problems of urban or suburban orientation. They are helping them "get off the streets and highways"—just as the hotels, a half century ago, had to move away from the noisy and smoky railroad terminals. They are suggesting areas for building where land use has been zoned thoroughly and, we hope, forever inviolably, for residence only—and with rigid controls placed on human density.

The living room of the Henry L. Kamphoefner house in Raleigh, North Carolina, shows the use of natural materials in the contemporary house. This development helped to humanize the almost antiseptic feeling engendered by the international style of the 1930's. The floor of this living room is made of pressed cork tile. The book cases and the wood of the end wall and the horizontal ceiling panel are of birch. The sloping ceiling is of lapped cypress boards, and the Roman brick walls are solid bearing walls. Three pairs of vertical doors at the far end of the room are of Philippine mahogany; they cover a series of horizontal wood louvres which permit natural air circulation without destroying privacy. A large plate-glass window wall is immediately opposite the long divan and affords an excellent view of the rolling topography of a golf course. The rugs in the room are old Navajo, in pleasant harmony with the natural modern materials. (*Henry L. Kamphoefner, Architect*)

*Plate I*

Since World War II more than thirty thousand Goodman "production-type" houses have been designed and built from coast to coast. Coming from the imagination of a careful and resourceful architect, they have been designed with a view toward saving money for the owner by the skillful use of prefabricated units of materials. The units are made and assembled in shops by finish carpenters and put together on the site by rough carpenters. In the house shown here, which Architect Goodman designed for himself in Alexandria,

*Plate II*

Virginia, he uses a standard panel on an eight foot by ten foot millwork frame glued together on a jig table. The frames are varied, some filled with glass, some wood, some with glass doors and windows. These frames are set up to form the walls of the house. Wherever they adjoin each other they are splined into a vertical column for support of the roof. The whole framing system is tied together at the top with two continuous two inch by twelve inch beams. The roof rafters are then supported on these lintel beams. In Plate II one may see how spaciousness has been achieved without loss of privacy. And in Plate III may be seen one of the many experiments in materials and techniques which are characteristic of these thousands of houses—wood flooring has been used for both vertical siding and flooring (and in other parts of the house the same material has been used for ceilings). This house gives the lie to the concept that good houses cannot be built by volume designers. It could be said with more truth that many volume designers are not sufficiently talented or interested in good community planning and house design to come up with first-rate results such as this. (*Charles M. Goodman Associates, Architects and Engineers*)

*Plate III*

*Plate IV*

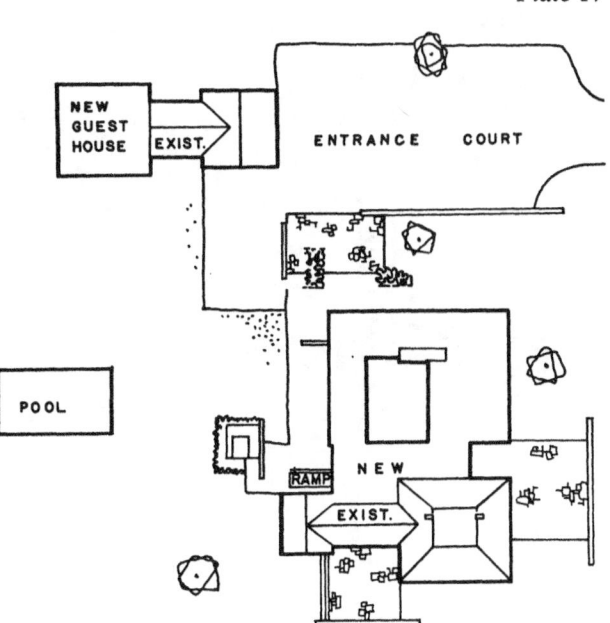

*Plate I*

*Plate II*

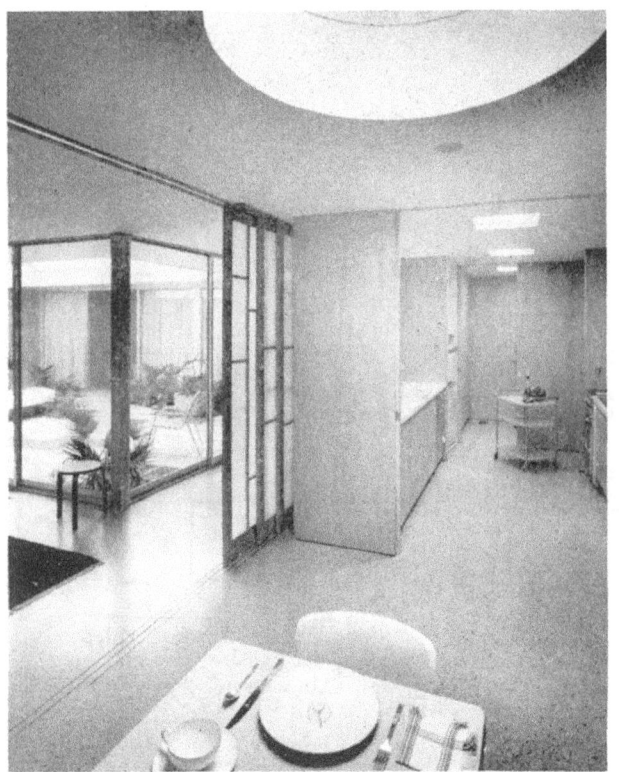

The Freedman town house in New Orleans was designed for an extremely restricted lot, and the architects have solved this limitation by developing the elements around a central, enclosed patio. It may be seen that the plan clearly defines the three main elements of the house and gives each its appropriate character—privacy in the bedroom wing, compact utility in the core of dining, kitchen, and laundry areas, and spaciousness in the living and guest area. Each area has a view of the patio, while a clever use of sliding screen walls ensures seclusion when necessary in the dining room, kitchen, and study. When opened, these sliding walls completely remove any feeling of the entrance hall's being a hall at all, because the study becomes one large area and the patio appears to be lengthened and to become one with the living room and the dining room and kitchen. Plate II shows a view across the dining table through the patio toward the bedroom wing which demonstrates the spaciousness achieved by the opening of the sliding doors. It is worth noting that privacy in the bedroom wing is achieved by the use of floor-length curtains along the plate glass walls. And, of course, when the curtains are opened, the space of the patio increases by the depth of the bedrooms which come into view. The same effect is achieved for those who are using the bedroom area. Also in Plate II one can see that the dining table is lighted in the day by a plastic skylight; this avoids the necessity of piercing the exterior walls and destroying privacy. The entrance front of the Freedman house is set back from the street in a simple paved and landscaped forecourt which is used as the entrance pathway to the large grille which has a gate at the right side for the main entrance. The carport on the left is adjacent to the kitchen for easy movement of groceries and supplies. The plan shows how cleverly the architects have placed the bathrooms and storage areas along the front wall to act as an extra sound baffle against street noise.

This house might be called a contemporary solution to the traditional patio house of the New Orleans Vieux Carré. However, while the architects have done a fine job of design within the limitations imposed upon them by the site, it is obvious in examining the site plan that there were so-called modern zoning restrictions on all sides. The strips of land entrapped in the imposed arbitrary land setbacks are lost to the owner and designer as usable land. This example points up the archaic zoning imposed on city lots by some well-intentioned real estate developers and city officials. (*Lawrence, Saunders, and Calongne, Architects*)

*Plate III*

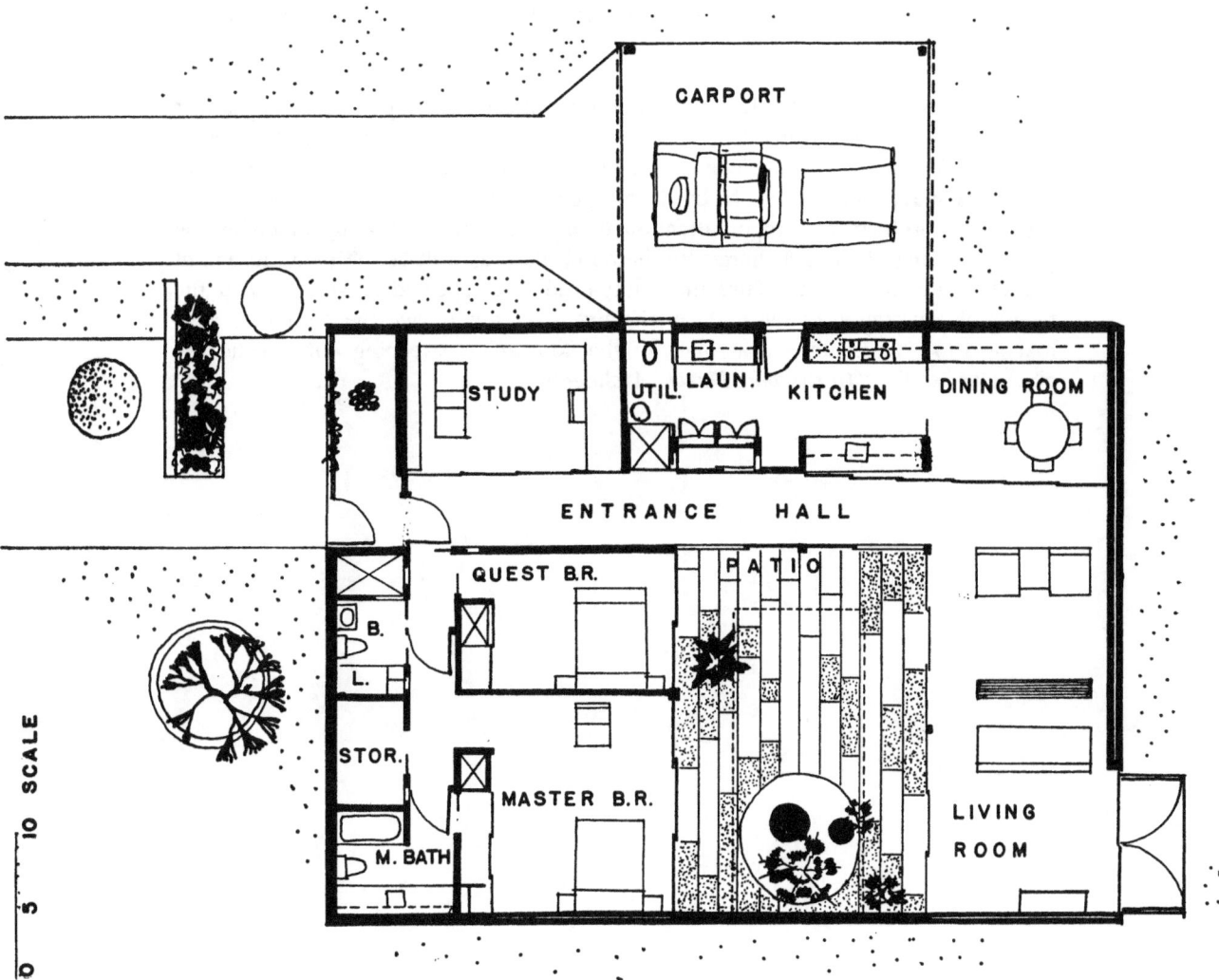

*Plate I*

This week-end house done for the Shushan family in Louisiana demonstrates how a simple post- and beam-structure can support the roof rafters, permitting large plate-glass windows to be inserted directly. The plate glass is not broken up with opening sash or sliding doors: jalousies for ventilation are placed at the lower edge of the central plate-glass wall, and doors with glass jalousies are located at each end of the plate-glass wall to give ventilation and access to the garden area. The architects have carried the stone pavers out one course beyond the glass wall to give a sense of continuity and then changed to an open-jointed paving slab for the covered porch area. The house shows a clean use of the plate-glass window wall with proper protection from sun glare by adequate overhang and the use of heavy natural planting.

One of the problems of the plate-glass wall in architectural design resides in the fact that although in the daytime it may be a great colorful mural, at night it becomes a black cold void. A house which appears spacious in the daytime may have to retract its space feeling at night by draping out the void. Curtis and Davis have solved this problem by proper attention to night lighting. The lights under the porch overhang (Plate II) illuminate the porch floor as well as the planting box at the left end of the house. Thus the plants inside are repeated outside, so that the feeling of penetration of the night is effective. By this device the architects have managed to give an illusion at night of the floor space sweeping out beyond the plate-glass wall. (*Curtis and Davis, Architects*)

*Plate II*

The town-house residence of Sam B. Short, Jr., in Baton Rouge, Louisiana, is placed on a corner lot fifty feet wide by one hundred and twenty feet deep. The owner-architect's program for the house, based on the needs of a family of three with accommodation for an occasional overnight guest, provides three bedrooms and pullman-type bath with small dressing room spaces at each end, kitchen, dining, and living room, and, finally, a carport with an architectural studio. The design here might be said to have been derived from a structural formal approach, but it is handled by an architect who could develop it with complete freedom. The

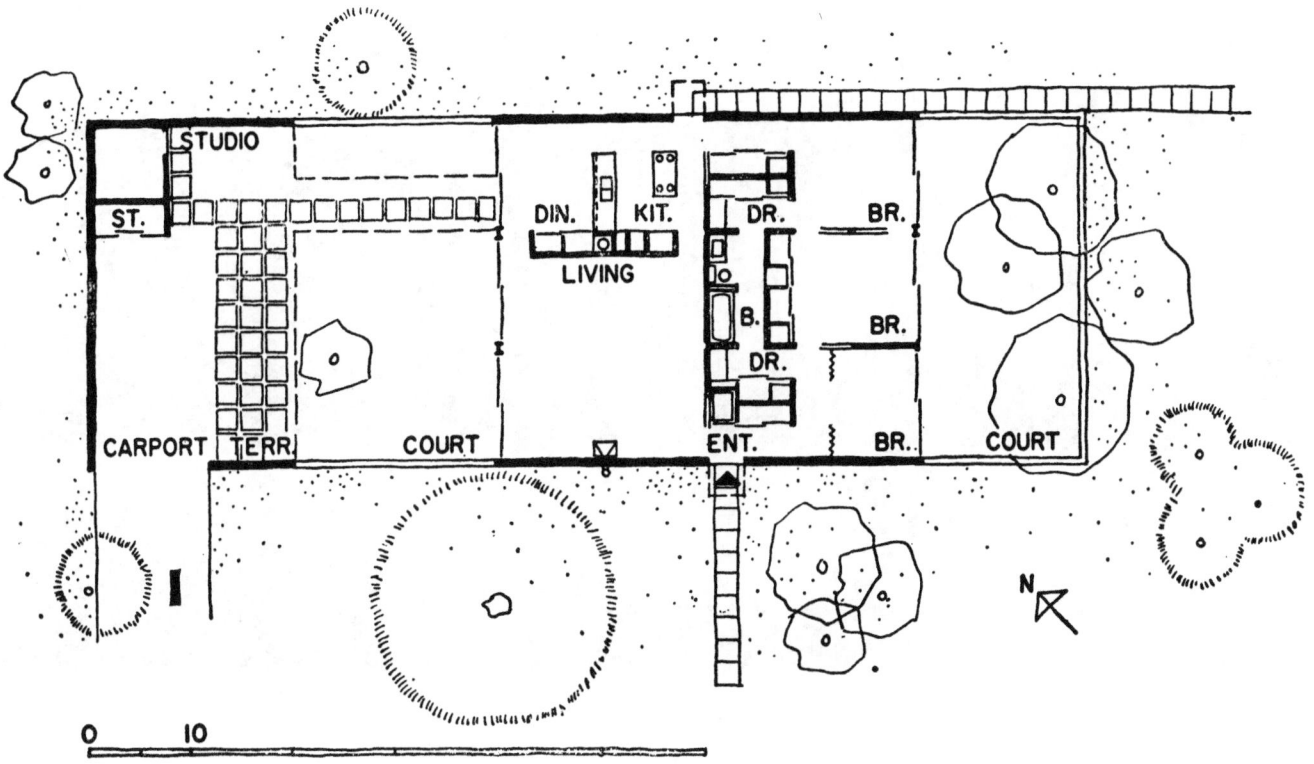

main theme is readily discernible in the triple arched shells which cover the carport and studio, repeated after a space interval for an outdoor living court in the covering of the living room and main house. The whole is terminated by another space interval, the bedroom court. The block masonry walls which surround the entire site are pierced at minimum points for carport and kitchen entrances. The enveloping nature of this wall assures a unity of purpose for the whole design. The stacked block wall produces a light rhythm with the main supporting columns of the structure subtly interwoven to produce a harmonious unity. (*Short and Murrell, Architects*)

The Harkey residence in Pascagoula, Mississippi, is a beach house on the Gulf Coast. It backs up to a sloping site and therefore is partly two levels and partly one level. A modular rhythm of light steel columns has been developed here which achieves a delicate yet not spindly effect in the whole form of the building. A light fast-beat tempo, rather than the pounding chord of the large structural bay and the heavy column, has been used to develop a delicate façade. This house accents the difference between its modern structural system and that of the early Georgian house. The Georgian house of wood construction had solid wood knee-braces which were concealed by clapboard, while this house is braced laterally along its window facade by crossed steel tension rods which become the variation in its rhythmic beat. It shows that structural formalism can display a lightness in design which is a welcome change from the dead seriousness with which contemporary architects often take themselves and their designs. (*Curtis and Davis, Architects*)

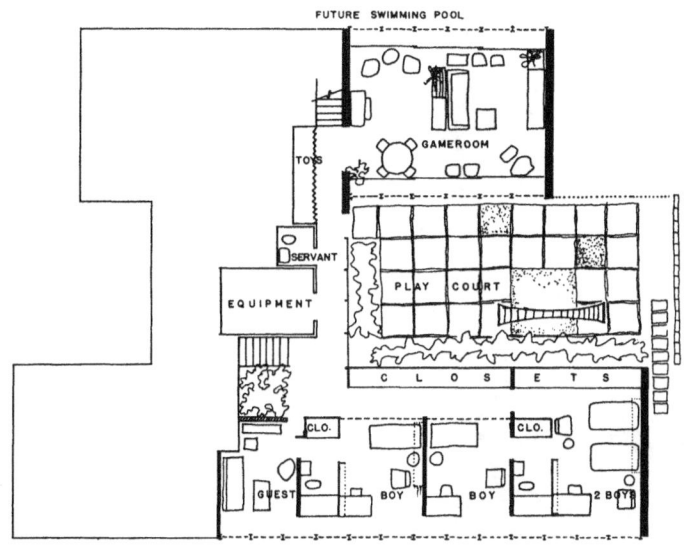

GROUND FLOOR LEVEL

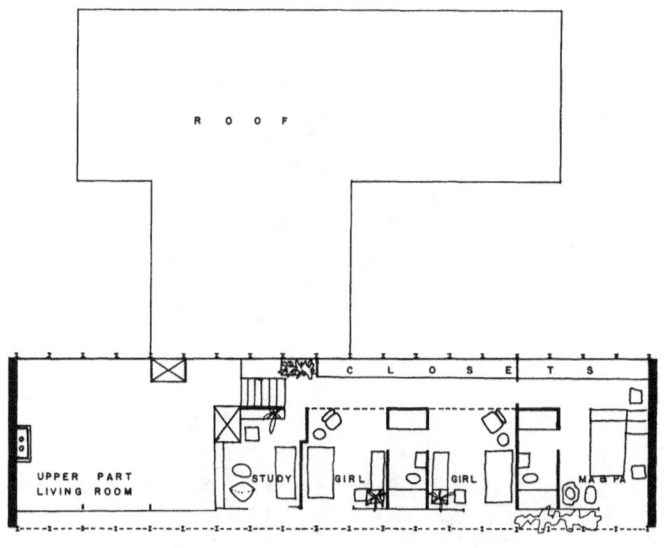

UPPER LEVEL

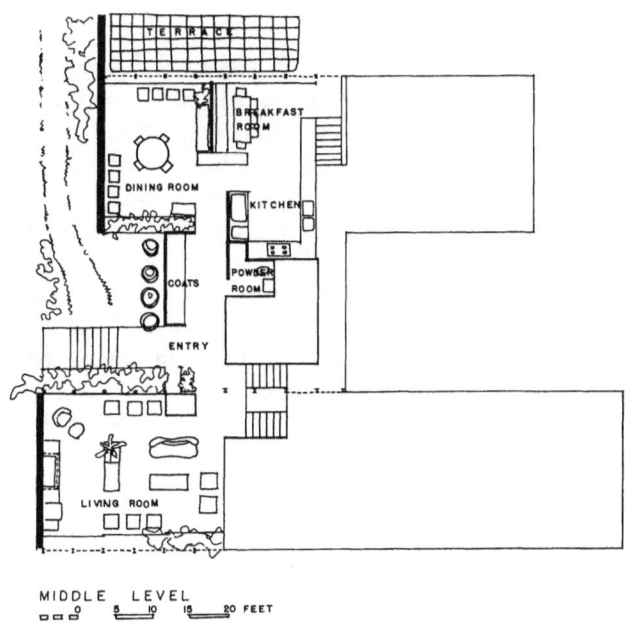

MIDDLE LEVEL

The spaciousness of this suburban residence of Cecil Alexander in Atlanta, Georgia, is a welcome contrast to the grudging approach imposed upon architects by clients insisting that every square foot serve some "practical" purpose. It is located on a sloping site, the upper side of the slope being the entrance side; the main entrance passes through the outer ring of the doughnut-shaped plan to the "hole" of the doughnut. And one feels upon entering that he is coming into a Roman atrium, the roof of which is a star-shaped folded plate appearing to float over its slender supporting columns. The triangular clerestory windows and the circular plastic dome give an incredible sense of living in the open in a substantially built house. There is a magnificent view across the living room to the woods. The house is one of the rare examples in which an architect has taken a powerful constructivist form and used it with skill to dramatize without letting the form dominate the entire space enclosed. (*Finch, Alexander, Barnes, Rothschild, and Paschal, Architects*)

Upper Floor Plan
1. Carport
2. Entrance
3. Living-Dining Room (20 x 42*)
4. Dining
5. Outdoor Dining Deck
6. Kitchen (18 x 14*)
7. Laundry (13 x 9*)
8. Maid (10 x 14)
9. Storage
10. Bedrooms (12 x 18*)
11. Guest room (12 x 18*)
12. Master Bedroom (19 x 14*)
13. Study (8 x 9)
14. Dressing Room

*Dimensions are average arcs.

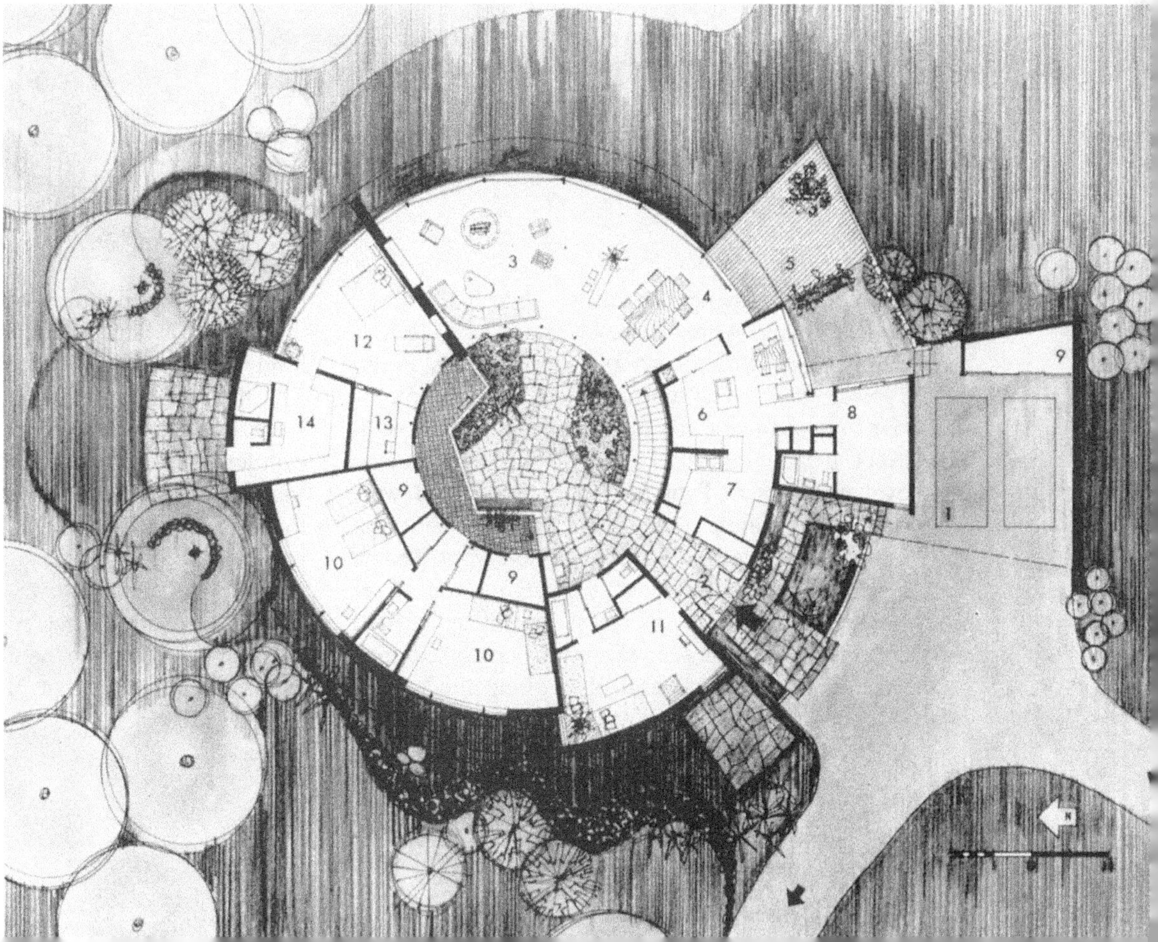

Plate I

The Matsumoto residence in Raleigh, North Carolina, is a two-level house with a three-bedroom housing unit on the upper level and a carport and architect's studio on the lower level. The house is a refined example of the order imposed by structural formalism in its design. The street façade (Plate I) gives privacy by having high-level windows to light the upper floors and windows under the cantilevered main floor to light the studio at the lower level. Six twelve-inch wood beams rest on a concrete block masonry wall on the street side of the house. Each of these beams is carried through to the garden façade, where it is supported once in the center of the house and once along the garden façade by wood columns. The columns supporting these floor beams are carried on through the upper level to support six matching twelve-inch roof beams. The floor joists and roof joists run across these main structural beams to cantilever at either end. These end cantilevers are expressed in the façade by treating the overhangs at either end with vertical wood siding while the remainder of the façade is developed with simple paneling with a glazed entrance in the center. This architect understands twentieth-century technology both in his use of prefabricated paneling and in the way he has integrated the mechanical equipment into the structural system. (*George Matsumoto, Architect*)

*Plate II*

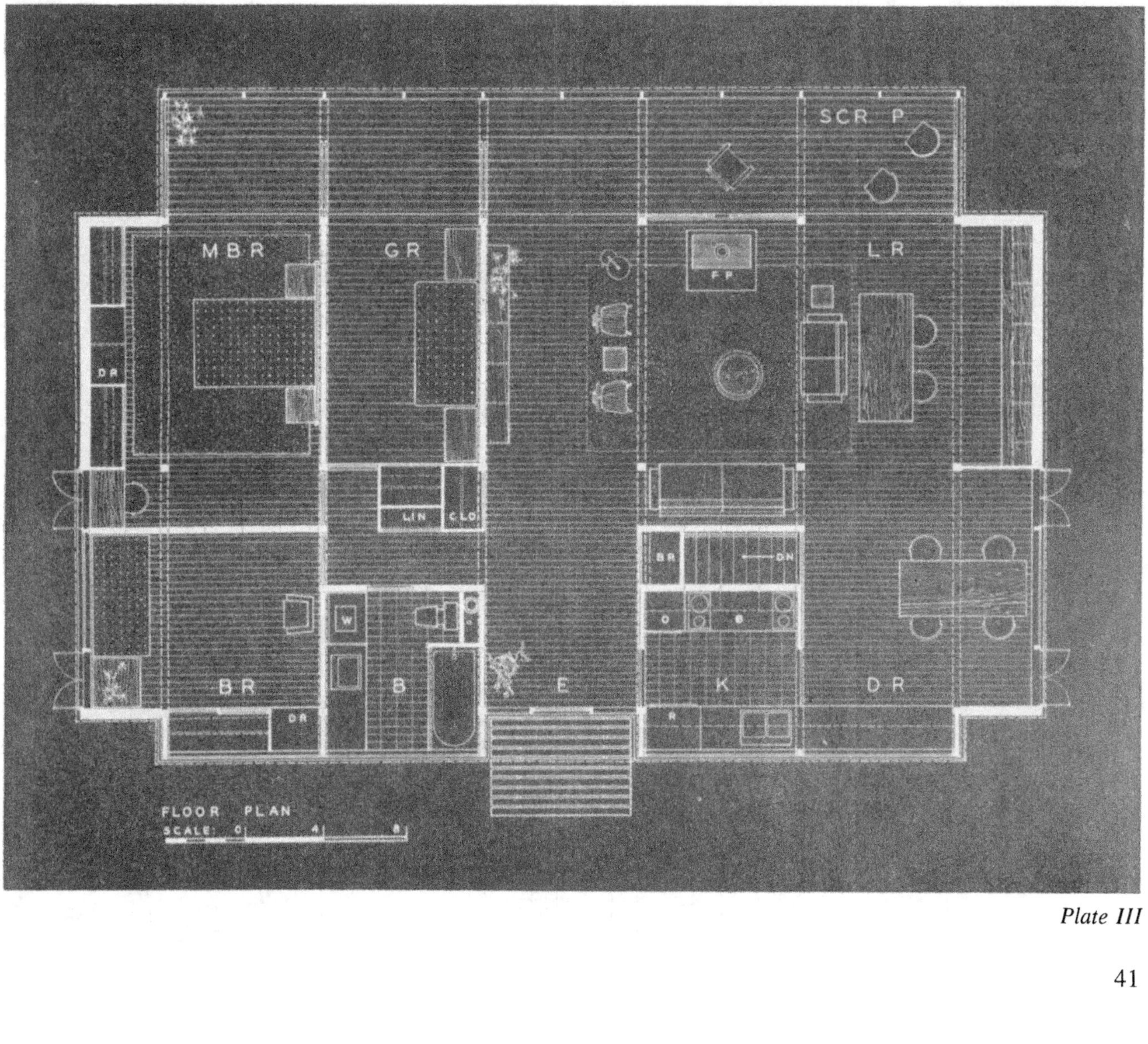

*Plate III*

Plate I

The ingenious design of this Knoxville, Tennessee, mountain house was influenced by the shortage of building materials after World War II. The architect happily combined available surplus quonset ribs with local discards from a nearby marble-veneer quarry to produce the basic roof structure and walls. The modular, four-foot spacing of the arched ribs was bridged by wooden blocking so that the roof sheathing and lathing for plaster might be attached. Full design advantage was taken of the modern architectural concept which insists that materials must be honestly expressed. Where steel ribs were exposed they were painted and left undisguised. Exposed masonry walls are used as terraces and as the spandril wall which protects the living room from the lower slope of the mountain side. Plate I shows how dramatically the architect has played up the light steel frame of the quonset ribs against the heavy, cairn-like terrace masonry seen on the left. In Plate II it will be seen that the house has two major floor levels, the lower accommodating the living area, the upper the sleeping rooms. In order to emphasize the full sweep of the arching roof, the master bedroom appears as an open balcony overlooking the living room, privacy being achieved by the use of draw draperies. The house is well sited and seems to grow out of the mountain side. In its mannerisms it is reminiscent of Frank Lloyd Wright and Bruce Goff. It lends the romantic impression that perhaps the architect has built a modern steel structure on an existing primitive ruin. (*James W. Fitzgibbon, Architect*)

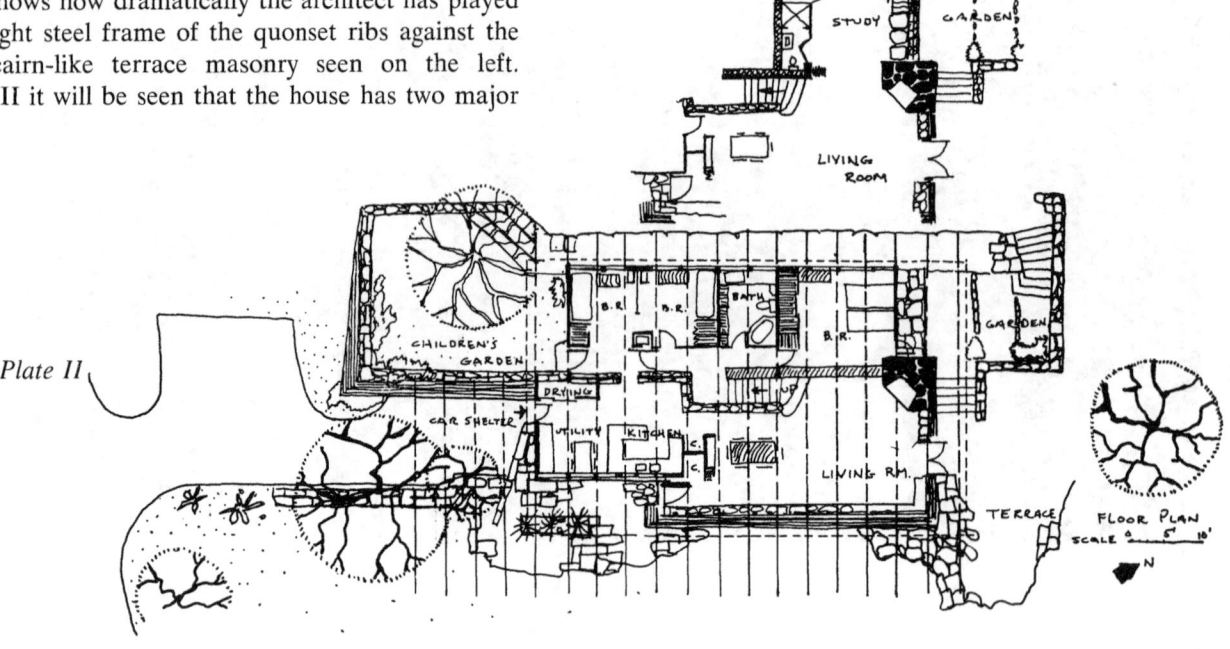

Plate II

# III. *The Contemporary Southern School*

AS stated in Chapter I, the reaction to the PWA school in the 1930's was so strong in the South, particularly in North Carolina, that it generated a new departure in the approach to school design. This departure took the form of an organic, social approach in architectural thinking. It manifested itself first in the design of the elementary school, worked itself up to that of the high school, and in the late 1950's reached that of the colleges.

The prime concept of this philosophy was the assumption that the first grader was a miniature-sized person, his sixth-grade counterpart was a middle-sized person, and so on. The idea that children are people, with different needs at different ages, was not limited to the study of the physical aspects of education but affected thinking about the psychological aspects as well. For example, the architect was faced with the problem of keeping the pint-sized school child from feeling overpowered by the authoritarian air of a building which he visited four hours a day as his first regular experience in time spent away from his family and home.

In most school districts of the South the school program is based either upon an eight-grade elementary school with a four-year high school or on a six-grade elementary school, a three-grade junior high school, and a three-grade senior high school. Architects and school officers, working in collaboration and receiving guidance from divisions of school planning operated by state departments of public instruction, began by making certain elementary breakdowns. For example, in a six-grade elementary school it was felt that the first three grades should be separated as an age group and the upper grades should be called, as distinct from the primary group, the grammar group. This then suggested dividing the elementary school architecturally into its two major educational elements. It was logical to separate these two elements by the third element, which needed to be accessible to both—the library, administration offices, cafeteria, auditorium-gym, and music and special study rooms.

The individual classroom is regarded by the contemporary architect as one of a series of beads strung on a main string of circulation to make up the total school. The organic approach is particularly felt in the careful analysis which is made of the child's school day as he would spend it at each grade level. For example, first graders would have to have a much larger area in which to operate as a group than sixth or seventh graders because of the shortness of their attention span. First-grade activities range from reading, writing, dancing, playing, graphic arts, and modelling to instruction on how to go to individual room toilets and how to check personal appearance. While all these varied activities might take place in the primary child's room and an adjoining outdoor classroom, the sixth grader might move to different areas for many of his activities. Furnishings, both fixed and movable, relative in size to the child's age become important elements from which the space design is created.

As a child becomes more advanced in the educational process, so the classroom needs to become more specialized. By the time the child reaches high school, specialized teachers are attached to various specialized rooms in departmentalized groupings which have become almost standard in the South. However, in some larger Southern high schools the student body is sometimes broken down into smaller organic groups, each consisting of different age levels. These groups are housed in satellite buildings complete with academic rooms, activity rooms, general science areas, and even branch libraries. These building groups are then interrelated with administration offices, auditorium, cafeteria, and main library. Another important contribution which has been made by the architect has been in persuading school authorities that the high school should be developed for the tax-paying community and opened for general recreation and other uses from twelve to eighteen hours a day. In a few of the larger cities such developments are taking place, and high-school libraries frequently are open from eight to ten at night daily through Sundays.

The better contemporary schools in the South often illustrate the contribution made by the architect in meeting the complex building needs of evolving curricula and in designing for flexible multi-use of spaces and areas and for probable future expansion. Improvement in the physical environment, from both a functional and an aesthetic point of view, frequently stimulates school administrators and teachers to more imaginative thinking about the teaching program.

At the same time, good school buildings must be integrated into their sites and into their neighborhood environments if they are to function completely. This involves landscape design of the site for outdoor school activities as well as provision for easy pedestrian access. Approaches should be well protected from all automobile traffic in and around the school area. This last requirement is rarely met in the urban and suburban school because of the inability of the architect to control the planning of the over-all environment. In the rural areas of the South most students commute by school bus—a circumstance that affects the site planning of country schools.

An important development in rural areas is the fast change from the system of many one- and two-teacher schools to the consolidated school pattern. The consolidated high school gives the rural student the opportunity of an enriched curriculum made possible by the larger faculty. Many architects have been of great help to school boards in convincing rural communities of the advantages of having their children attend modern consolidated schools, even though extended bus rides prolong the school day.

A good public school, then, is one which functions internally while at the same time it relates itself to its over-all environment. As the better architects continue to strive for better design solutions, both functionally and aesthetically, it is regrettable to note that many of the new schools, while modern in general character, are drab and stereotyped in their designs.

In higher education the progressive architect throughout the nation is now facing new challenges, arising from a simultaneous population explosion and rapid expansion of modern technology. By 1967 the huge crop of post-World War I babies will reach college age. Colleges will be called upon to handle a doubling of their student enrollment at the same time that they face a comparative shrinking of manpower in the thirty-to-forty-year age group from which well-trained college teachers would have to come.

The development of higher educational programs has to be planned on a regional and state basis in a way that will avoid unnecessary duplication of curricular offerings and research projects. Perhaps many more junior colleges will have to be built in order to provide terminal education for some and the first two years of college for those who will go to the greater universities for degree courses. The local junior college will help solve the student housing problem, in that many students would be able to live at home for at least the first two years.

The horizontally designed campus comprised of two- and three-story academic and dormitory buildings is becoming less feasible in urban and semi-urban areas because of the fast-developing land shortages brought about by increased population, urban sprawl, and heavier automobile traffic. Furthermore, the large amount of land used for student and faculty parking is causing too much spread of the campus buildings, thus increasing circulation time between classes. Already the shortage of land is being solved architecturally by the use of multistory dormitories. Beginnings, too, are being made in the design of more compact classroom and laboratory buildings. Because of the shortage of experienced faculty referred to above, the need for larger classes will have to be recognized in the design of future college classroom buildings.

While entirely new campuses are beginning to appear in new smaller towns in the South (mostly sponsored by private groups such as churches), the real challenge is the expression of existing university campuses. A few of the larger universities are awakening to a recognition of these problems, but it will take the combined efforts of administrators, faculties, and architects to develop the criteria for a new design philosophy which will meet these needs.

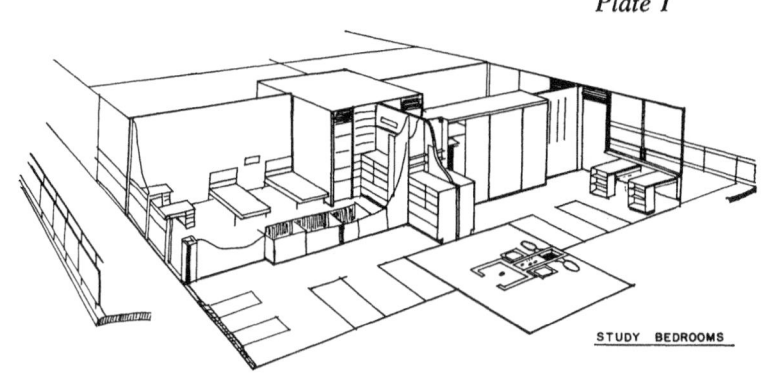

*Plate I*

STUDY BEDROOMS

This graceful mens' dormitory at Atlantic Christian College in Wilson, North Carolina, is successful architecture because the designer carefully allowed for all the requirements and limitations inherent in the design of such a facility. The most important functions of a dormitory are assuring conditions for good sleep and study, along with easy dressing and toilet arrangements. As seen in Plate I, four similar study-bedrooms are extremely well-organized around a central toilet core. Each has direct access to the toilet and to the peripheral corridor balconies (Plate II). These balconies, handsomely integrated into the structure of the building, not only provide circulation but achieve the necessary overhangs for sun control. The first floor of the building is used for public rooms and outside entrances. Vertical circulation is obtained by stairways which are connected to the peripheral balconies (Plate III). (*Small and Boaz, Architects, Joseph N. Boaz, partner in charge*)

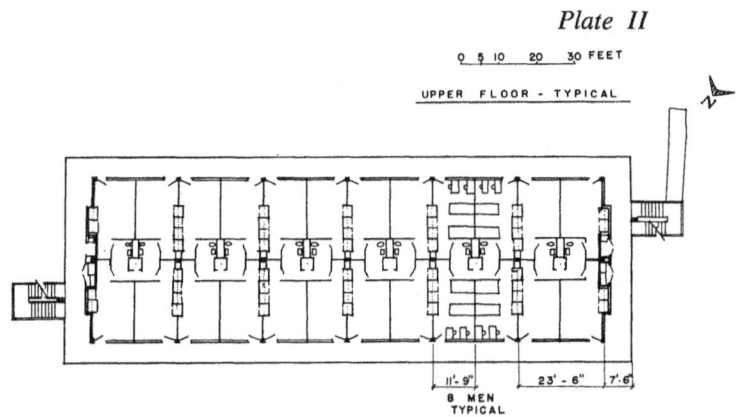

*Plate II*

UPPER FLOOR - TYPICAL

8 MEN TYPICAL

*Plate III*

The Thomy Lafon School, an elementary school in New Orleans, indicates a new direction in school design which, it is hoped, will be followed in other places, perhaps even in California. The California architect is responsible for the pavilion type of school which, because of its open, spreading plants, used up land at an alarming rate—land which we do not have any more in urban areas. The school board of New Orleans and some school architects are taking a realistic view of the

population expansion in the United States by raising their schools above the ground so that the areas beneath the schools may be used as playgrounds. This is an important development when one considers that this makes good play areas sheltered from rain and the Southern sun. While the classrooms of the school are kept on the upper level, the main service elements are located centrally in a one-story unit, part of which appears to slide under the elevated classrooms. This central unit provides the library, the principal's office, the multipurpose room, the auditorium-cafeteria, and the kitchen. Also, toilets are strategically located under the elevated classrooms with stairs approaching them from above, readily usable from playground and classroom. The ramp at the end of the building guarantees an easy ascent to the upper level for handicapped children and a fast ascent for the able-bodied. (*Curtis and Davis, Architects*)

47

*Plate I*

*Plate II*

Plate III

The Wilson Junior High School in Mecklenburg County, North Carolina, can be described as an authentic twentieth-century design for junior high schools both because of its plan arrangement and its structural method and system of erection. It provides for grades seven, eight, and nine and allows for six general classrooms in each grade level. Each grade level has its separate cluster of classrooms with its own toilet facilities. An attractive courtyard connects these units to the central administration and library. Beyond are located science and home-making classrooms. A clever cafeteria design provides a walk-through kitchen cafeteria line and a circular multi-purpose room for the seating area. This also does duty as

Plate IV

a small auditorium for the school. Most of the building elements, including the structural system, are shop prefabricated. In the exterior views and the interior view down the corridor (Plate III) it should be noted how the panel walls have been developed with glass and with treated metal elements, as well as with steel school locker units. The basic structural system is made up of square steel columns and rectangular steel beams produced by welding two stair stringer channels together. The exterior walls of the building are either insulated metal panels or insulated porcelain-enamel panels with different colors in each wing. Prefabricated plastic skylights are also used strategically for good overhead lighting. The roof deck is made of pressed fibre plank which provides insulation and gives a pleasant acoustical surface. The building exhibits the refinement of detail and craftsmanship that can be achieved with well-detailed and carefully prefabricated machined parts. This would seem to be the twentieth-century architect's answer to those architects and would-be builders who lament the passing of the guild craftsman of the Middle Ages. (*A. G. Odell and Associates, Architect*)

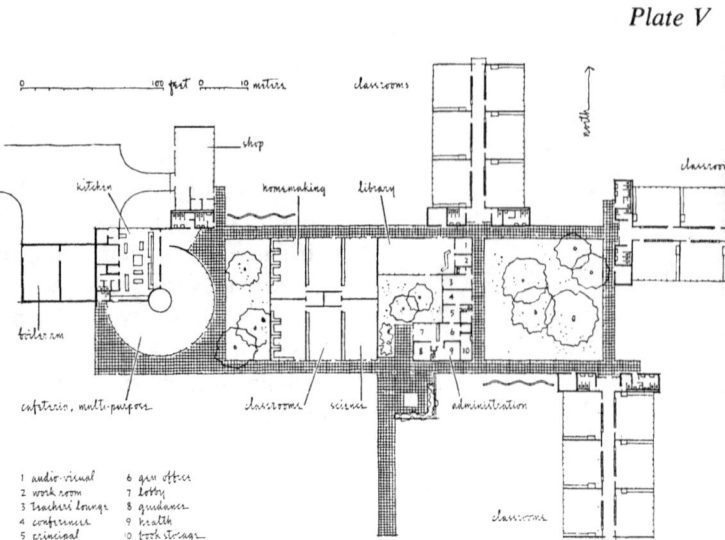

Plate V

50

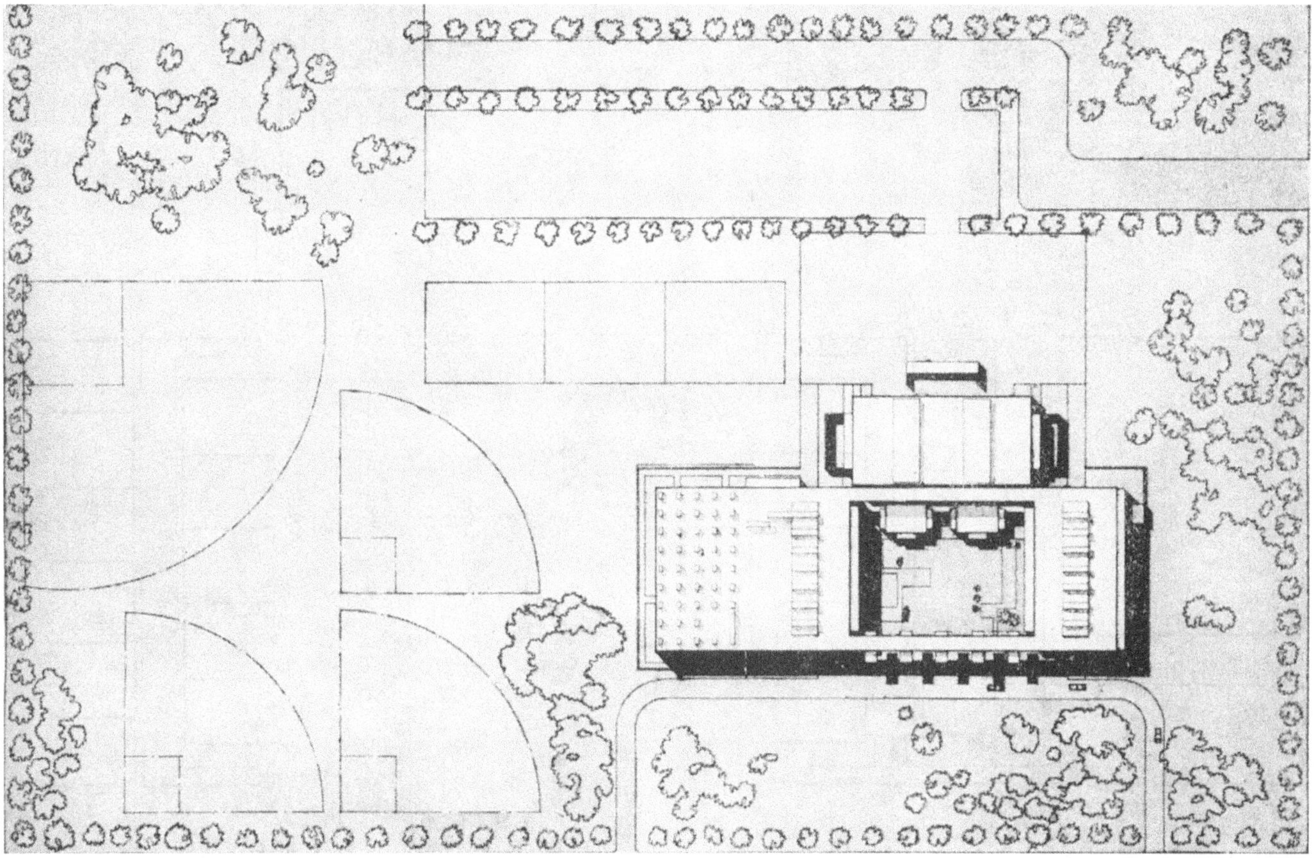

Riverview High School
Sarasota, Florida

*Plate I*

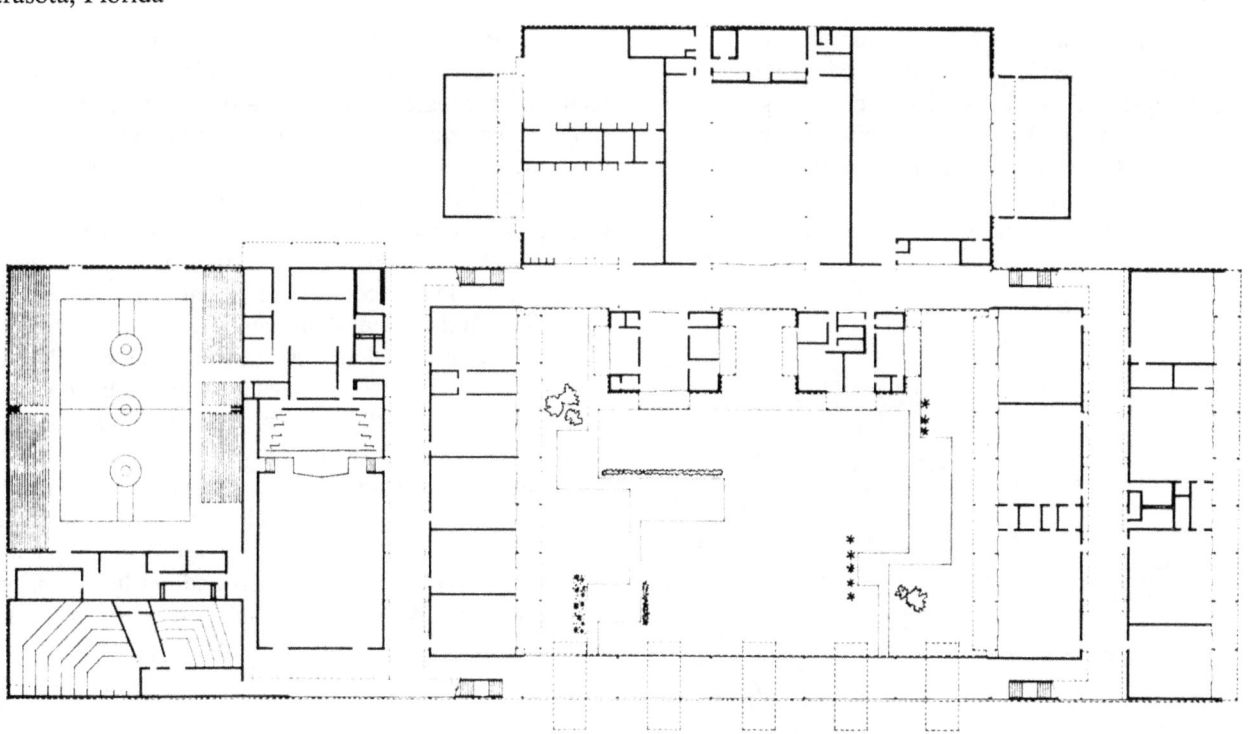

HIGH SCHOOL, SARASOTA, FLORIDA

*Plate II*

51

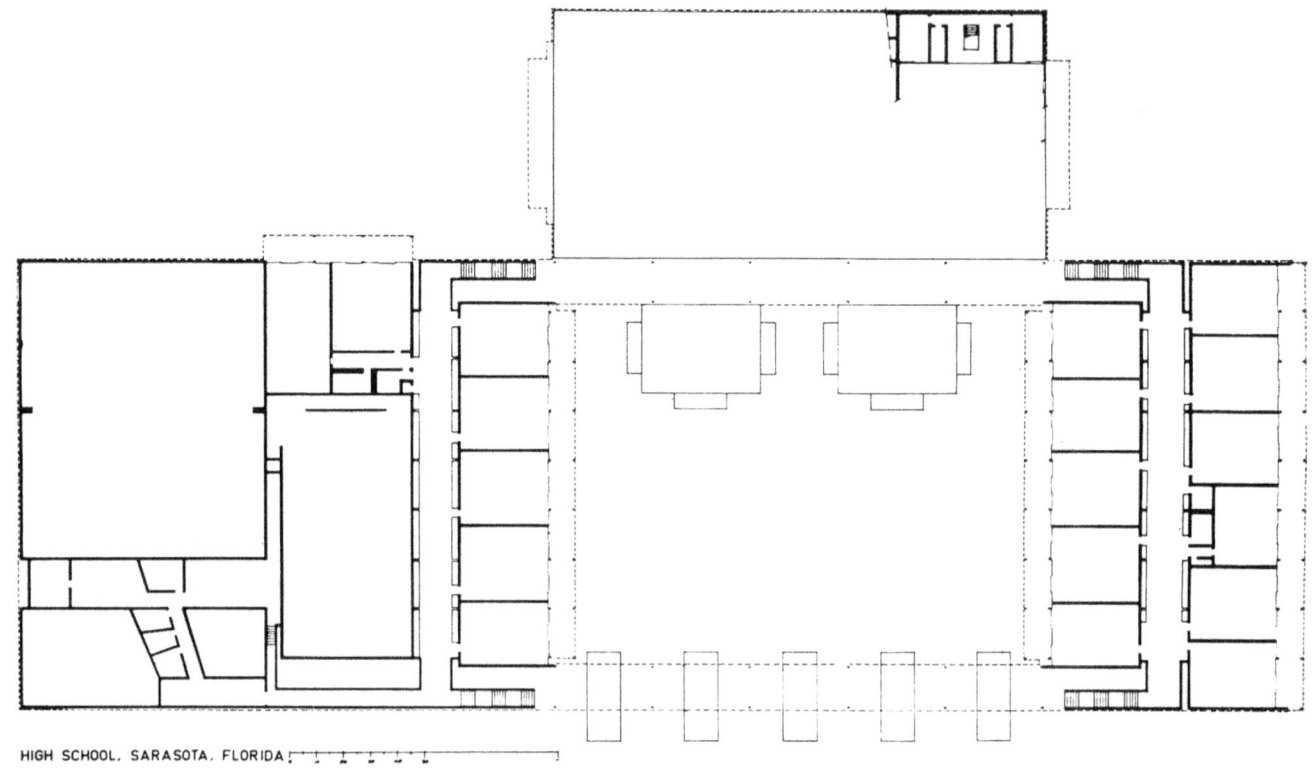

HIGH SCHOOL, SARASOTA, FLORIDA

*Plate III*

The Riverview High School, Sarasota, Florida, provides facilities for a complete secondary education. The building complex (Plate I) is placed on a large, flat, rectangular site giving pick-up automobile and bus access at the front of the building, while a landscaped parking area for 360 cars is placed well to the rear of the building. This leaves almost 40 percent of the site available for playing fields. The school building itself (Plates II and III) is organized for a departmentalized program grouped around an open quadrangle. The quadrangle is entered through a sweeping breezeway (Plate IV), with the auditorium, gymnasium, and music rooms to the left. A single-loaded classroom corridor of two stories completes this unit. At the back of the quadrangle is another group housing the cafeteria in the center. It is flanked on one side by design studios and shops and on the other by the library. Both of these last facilities have walled-in patios adjoining them for outside work. On the right of the quadrangle (Plate VI) are the science and homemaking laboratories with general classrooms above. The plan of this building is a welcome relief from the sprawling "finger" plans which have dominated the school designs of the 1950's. Architect Rudolph has achieved a masterful compactness and yet has managed to develop an open plan. Circulation routes are relatively short because of the decision to place cafeteria, library, and administrative offices in a central location.

*Plate IV*

*Plate V*

Design unity is developed by connecting the roof plane on the left to the roof plane on the right with high-level breezeways which give the quadrangle (Plate V) a space definition within the building group. The music department has been well zoned for audio isolation and yet it ties in well with the auditorium. Similarly, the shop and cafeteria are well zoned for their purposes. There is, however, some question about the library's being adjacent to the noisy cafeteria. The structural system of this building is steel frame and bar joist with acoustical plaster ceilings. Perhaps the building's most intriguing feature is the way the lightweight, precast canopies have been used to control sunlight and yet allow natural ventilation and clear vision through the glass walls. Delicately designed clerestory monitors allow light penetration into both the upper and lower inner corridors between classrooms. This was achieved by floating the second-story corridor as a bridge with space between it and the classroom corridor walls. The refined interplay of rhythms between the structural bays, the fenestration, and the sun canopies is expressed aesthetically in light and shade. But one wonders whether the high-level breezeways have any function other than the aesthetic, since as their height precludes their giving much weather protection. It is also doubtful whether so much exposed structural steel would pass the fire codes in many states. (*Paul Rudolph, Architect*)

*Plate VI*

Plate I

Many Virginians look back to the great days of Williamsburg and take a nostalgic pride in its recent restoration, but there are also those who try to look forward and design buildings in the twentieth-century idiom. The Princess Anne County High School, located not too many miles from Williamsburg, shows the acceptance of this point of view. On the building's right is the auditorium clearly recognizable by its form. To the left are the main two-story classroom wing and the bus-loading platform whose canopy also clearly expresses its purpose. (*Oliver and Smith, Architects*)

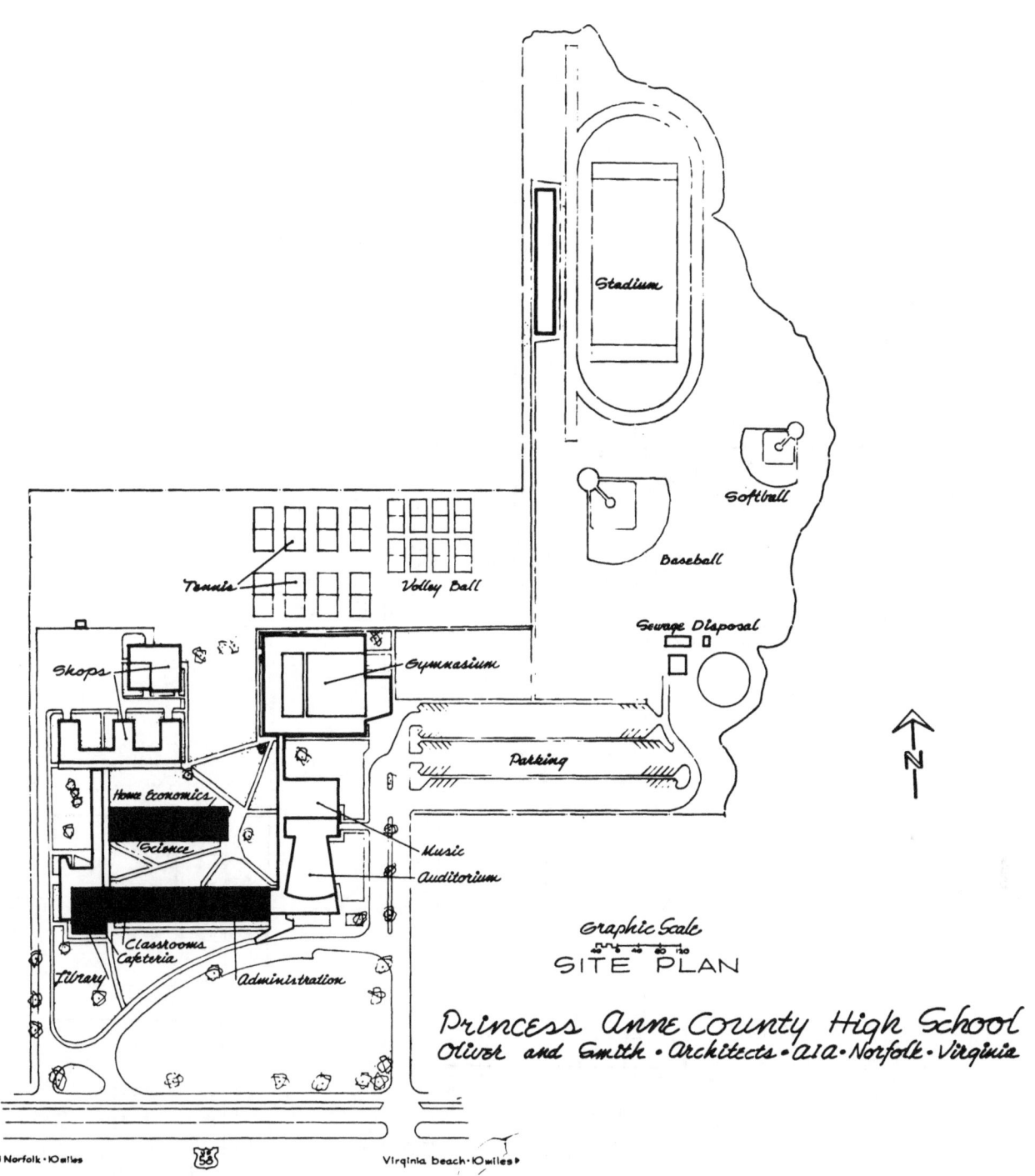

*Plate II*

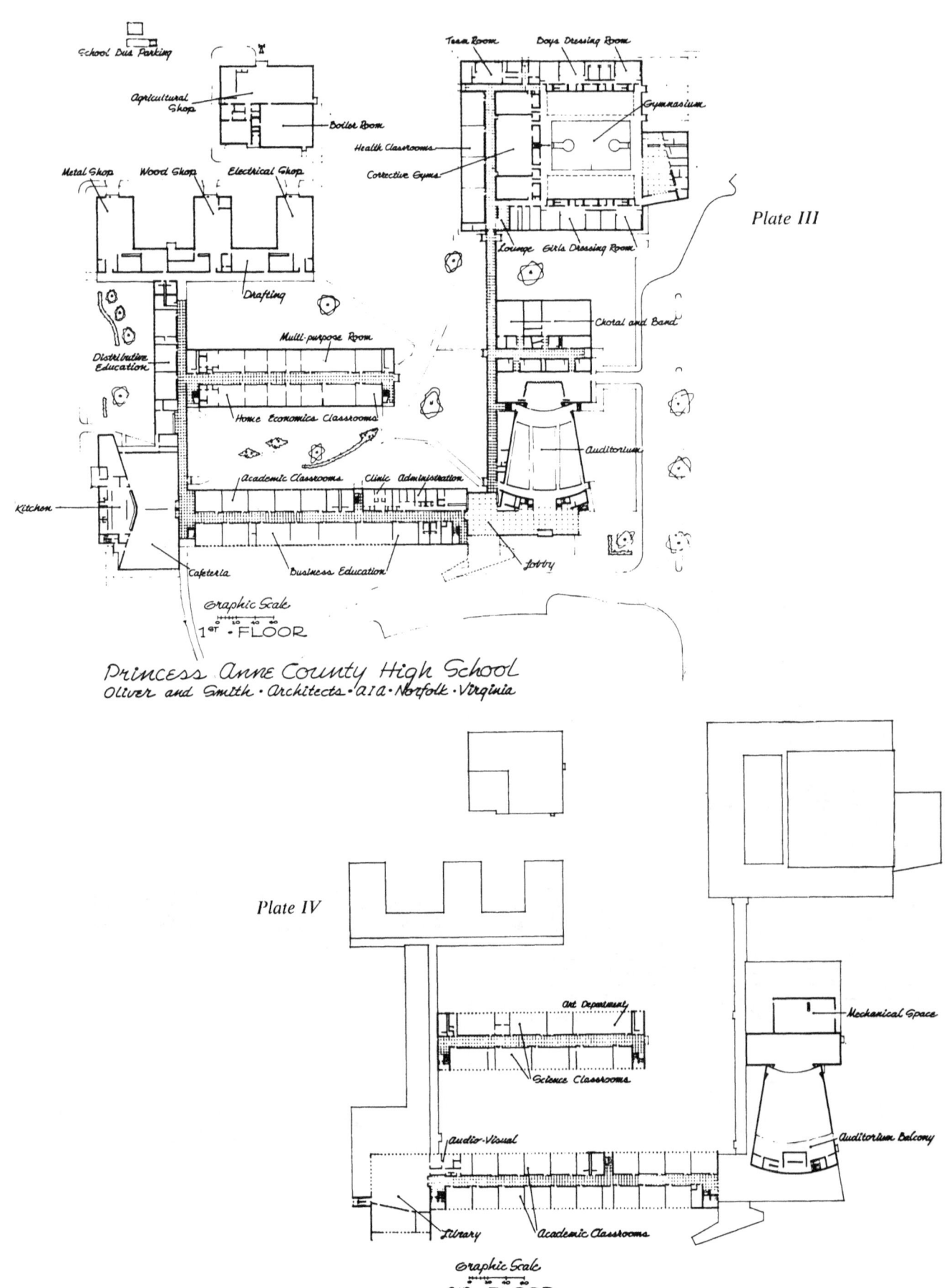

Florida Southern College at Lakeland, Florida, is unique both because it is being built from a master plan which was started in 1936 and because it is the largest aggregation of Frank Lloyd Wright buildings in the world. The organization of the campus (Plate I) places the chapel in the center, along with the library, administration building, a large pool, three seminar buildings, a music building, art museum, and studio buildings. At a greater distance from the center in various directions are manual training and domestic science buildings, along with an outdoor theater, swimming pool, faculty club, kindergarten, and science building. The most gratifying architectural aspect of the campus plan, however, is the fact that as far back as 1936 the parking was restricted to the periphery—and it is still restricted! In Plate II, the plan of the administration building shows the manner in which the esplanade penetrates through the administrative building group. In this feature of the design one senses an overtone of the medieval cloister. In Plate III, a view of the administration building, one may see the low height of the esplanade changing to the opposite as it meets the building—a dramatic effect to which Wright was addicted. This handling may be seen again in Plate IV, the E. T. Roux Library; and in Plate V, in which the students in the balcony appear to be bumping their heads on the ceiling. In this semicircular library the layers of disks which form the roof allow natural light to penetrate between the disks straight to the catalogue and main desk. Also in Plate V it may be seen that the structural members of the building appear both internally and externally. In Plate VI, the Danforth Chapel, the strong Japanese influence which Wright enjoyed playing with shows in his expression of the roof line and the large window. The building, however, manages to seem heavy because of the Victorian rustica-

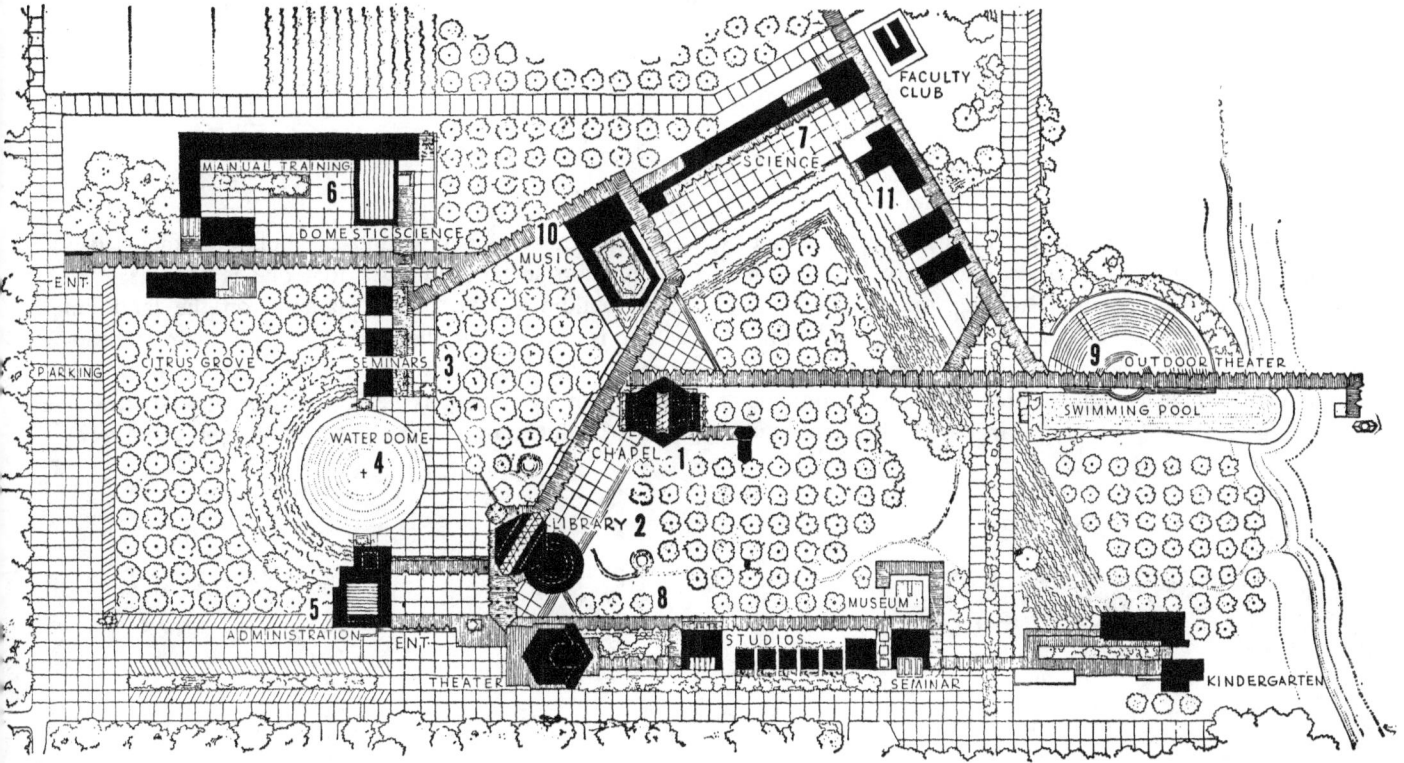

Florida State College
Lakeland, Florida

*Plate I*

Plate II

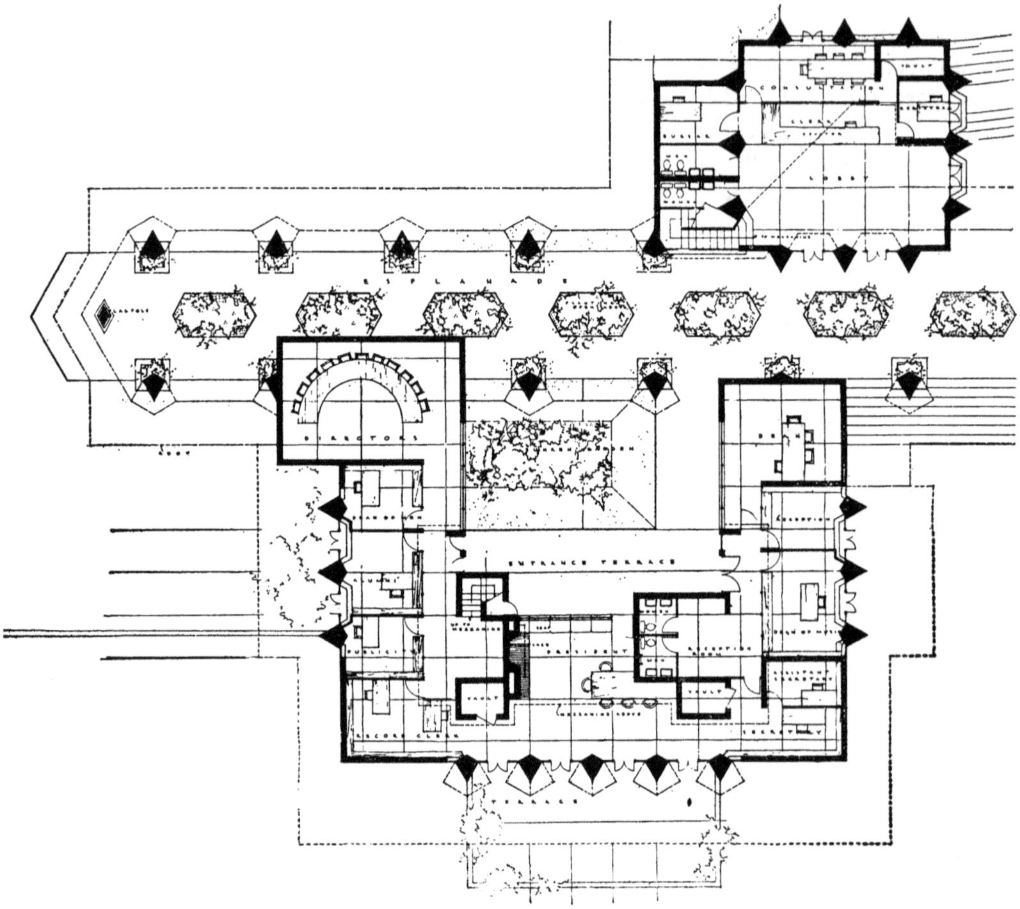

tion treatment of the masonry. In any case the whole building gives evidence of a strong creative hand. In Plate VII, the Polk Science Building, one may see the magic with which the buildings, landscaping, and walkways are woven together to produce an integrated whole —the whole which Wright so often described as organic architecture. The sculptural surface of the land, the planting, the esplanades, and the buildings themselves all function so harmoniously that one is unaware that these buildings have been "planted" on the land but rather is aware that they are one with their environment. The demonstration of this synthesis over and over again by Wright is perhaps his greatest contribution to architecture. (*Frank Lloyd Wright, Architect*)

Plate III

Plate IV

*Plate V*

*Plate VI*

*Plate VII*

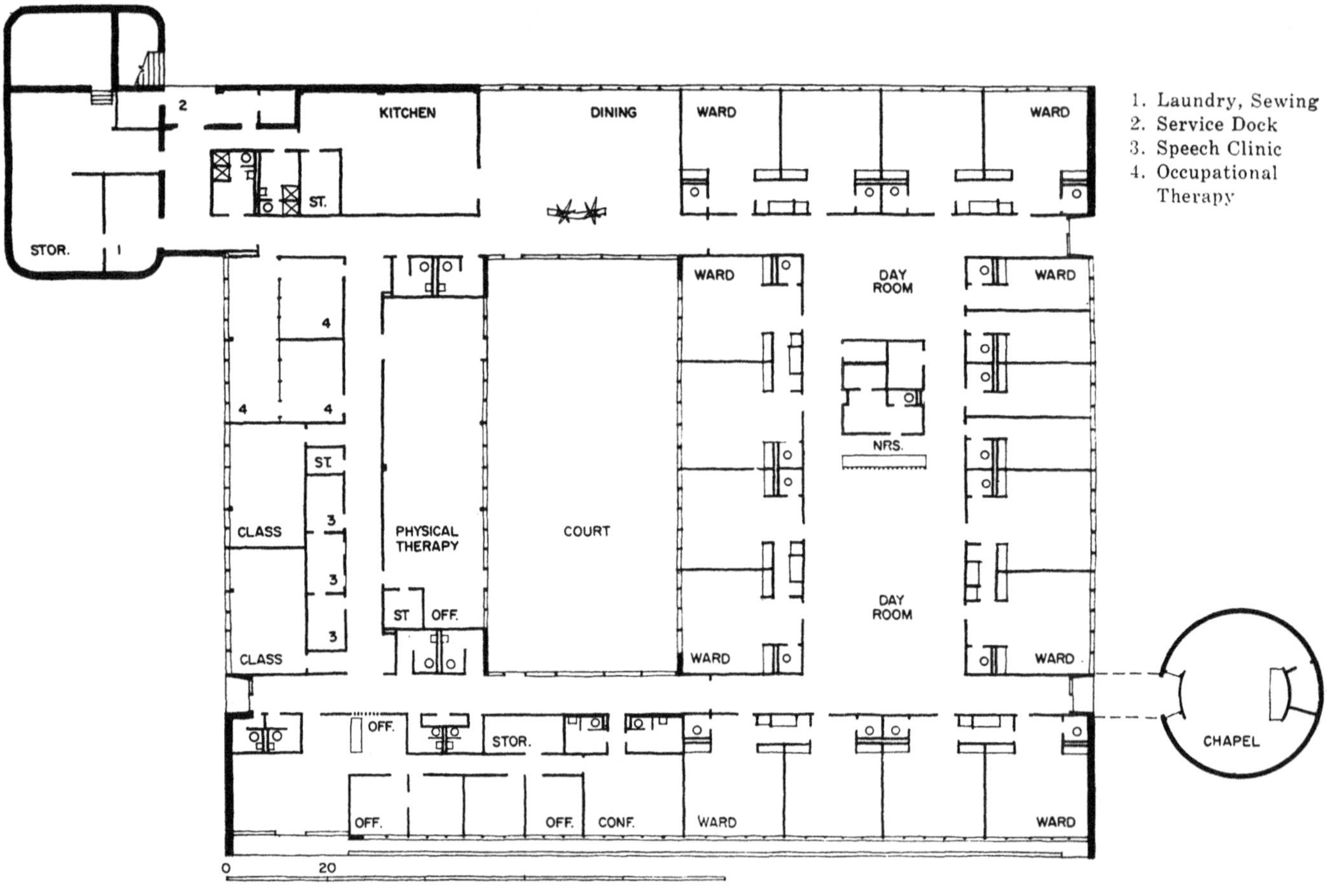

1. Laundry, Sewing
2. Service Dock
3. Speech Clinic
4. Occupational Therapy

*Plate I*

This hospital school in Jackson, Mississippi, is operated by the Mississippi Department of Education. It is a simple pavilion-like structure developed around an inner court. The purpose of the school is to rehabilitate cerebral palsied children. Since the therapy may take several years, children are housed in wards so that it is possible for them to measure their own problems against the problems of others in similar circumstances. The wards open off dayrooms, with a centrally located nursing station. For children who are able to be moved or who are semi-ambulatory there are classrooms, physical therapy rooms, and a speech clinic. There is also a small, detached chapel which is connected to the main building by a breezeway (Plate IV). Con-

*Plate II*

*Plate III*

tinuous window walls interspersed with solid masonry bearing walls make up the main treatment of the exterior façade. A simple concrete grille provides sun screening along the front (Plate II). The covered canopy over the main entrance is folded up at its front edge for an identification. This rather mars the simple lines of an otherwise good building. (*Biggs, Weir, and Chandler, Architects*)

*Plate IV*

Plate I

The College Union on the North Carolina State College campus in Raleigh is a three-level building with a ground-floor opening on a campus mall on the south side. Its first floor opens to the north and gives access to the main automobile artery. Under pressure from the university administration, an attempt was made to follow the tradition of the nineteenth-century Southern plantation house. The portico was therefore placed on the north side because the authorities felt that this was the "entrance" side of the building. In fact, the south side is the working entrance as far as the campus population is concerned. The resulting building defies the precepts of Vitruvius and Louis Sullivan by having its portico on the shaded side and a completely unshaded glass window wall on the south side. Summer glare and heat have been so unbearable that draperies remain continuously drawn as seen in the photograph in Plate II. The plan of the building, however, works extremely well. The architectural detailing is clean and well executed, and the building has a "happy" and pleasant atmosphere. It is in constant use by the student body as a campus social center. (*William Henley Deitrick, Architect*)

Plate II

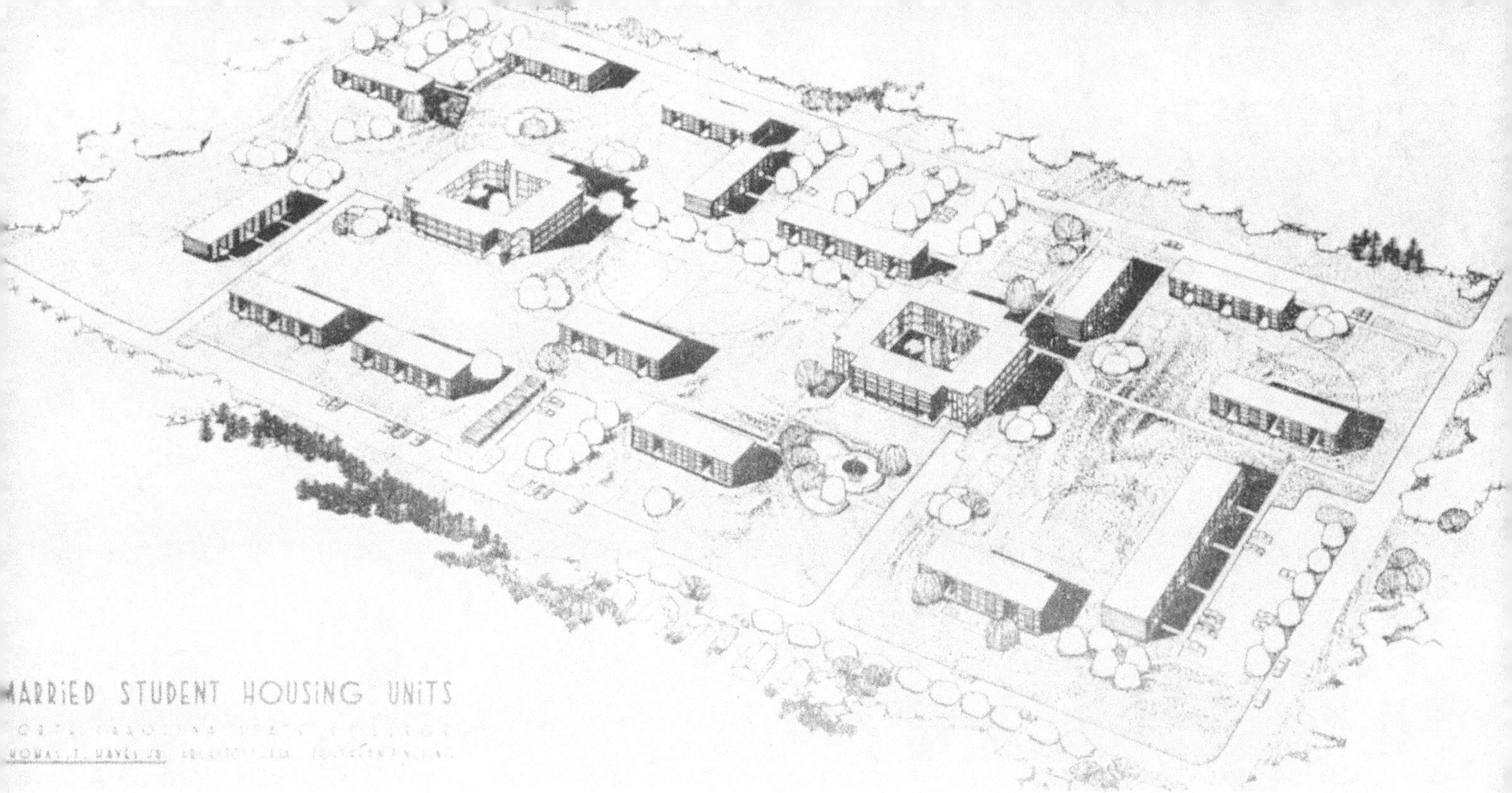

MARRIED STUDENT HOUSING UNITS

*Plate I*

Whether for better or for worse, since World War II married students and their families have become a familiar and important factor in all campus population measurements. These married students' housing units were designed for North Carolina State College at Raleigh and are to cost about two million dollars. The buildings will consist of three hundred units to be built on about half of the site available (Plate I); the complete project, to be finished later, will include up to six hundred units complete with schools and shopping center. In Plate I it may be seen that thirty-two two-bedroom apartments are grouped off to themselves, as it was expected that most of the students with children would be housed in these. The 148 one-bedroom units are therefore placed around the periphery of the present plan, and the 120 efficiency units are grouped around courts in the interior of the site. The units are well conceived in space and articulation (Plate II) and are designed to face into the site, while all parking and traffic are held to the periphery of the area. (*Thomas T. Hayes, Jr., and Associates, Architects*)

*Plate II*

A laboratory and classroom building for Christian Brothers College, Memphis, Tennessee. This building is the expression of a structural design enclosing delicate architectural forms. Brick has been used for the solid panel walls and also to give a tapestried effect in some of the balcony corridors. The architects have also used barrel-vaulted, covered walks to connect playfully the various buildings. The regular undulation of these vaulted walks enriches the campus by appearing to unify the new with the more traditional buildings into one master scheme. And, of course, for students and faculty, the walks afford good covered access to buildings. (*A. L. Aydelott and Associates, Architects*)

The architects of this dormitory at Oglethorpe University in Georgia used a residential scale and design approach in order to achieve informality in this dormitory lounge. The stone chimney in the center rises up as an obelisk-like shaft to pierce the sloping plane of the roof, which is supported by heavy timber beams. (The exterior of the building picks up the field stone of the chimney, and the use of windows slotted vertically makes an attractive rhythm, although perhaps it does cut down natural daylighting.) The fireplace has a depressed brick hearth with seating pads around its edge. This treatment is undoubtedly useful when the students are grouped around the fireplace for discussions. (*Toombs, Amisano, and Wells, Architects*)

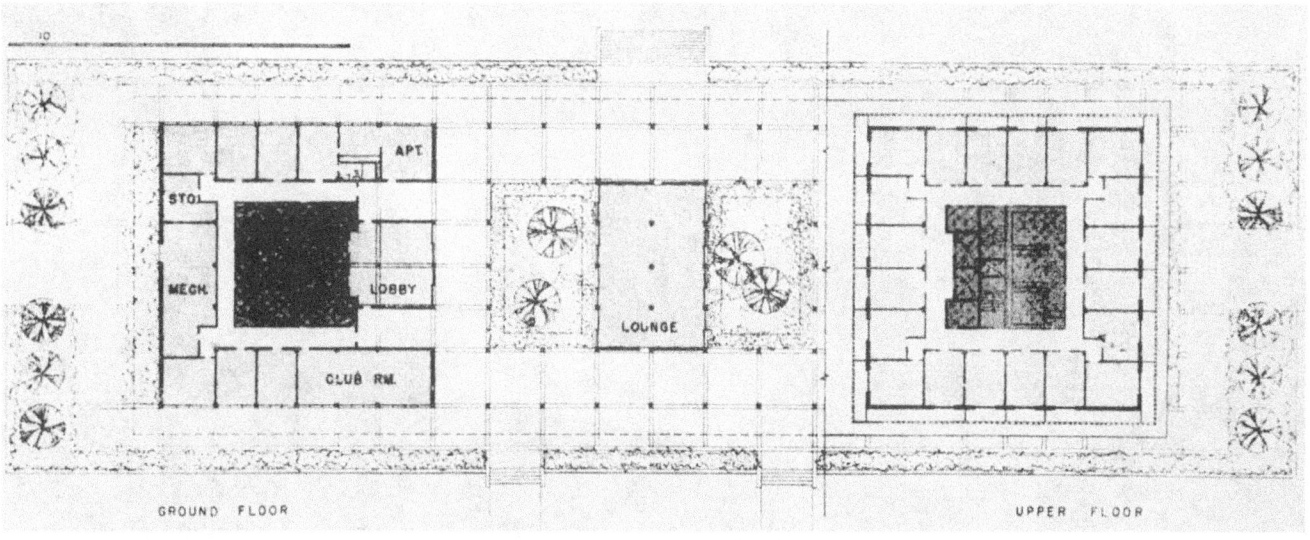

GROUND FLOOR  UPPER FLOOR

These University of South Carolina dormitories for men at Columbia show that South Carolina, which has an architectural tradition going back to Charleston's heyday, is not frustrated by nostalgic awe of the past. These two towers, representing the first part of a six-dormitory building program, are spaced side by side and are connected at ground level by a one-story pavilion structure which provides a central lounge. The lounge is flanked by open courtyards lighted through rectangular pierced openings in the roofs that allow the area to be landscaped. These buildings are square in plan and provide for twenty student rooms on the periphery of each floor, connected by an inner hall which surrounds a square utility space housing twin elevators, stairs, and toilet facilities. The first floor of each building accommodates the entrance lobby, counselor's apartment, club room, mechanical and storage rooms, and a few dormitory rooms. If these two towers had been treated with glass window walls on each façade, they would have appeared as glass cubes reminiscent of the international style. However, the architects have sheathed them in an envelope of pierced concrete grillwork which screens a series of galleries around the entire building, protected from the sun's direct rays. It also gives the building a constantly shifting play of light as the sun's position changes. This dramatic but simple solution is bold, clear, and uncompromising in achieving its purpose and is an important trend in contemporary architecture. (*Harmon, Stone, and Keenan, Architects*)

*Plate I*

These two plates show the extent to which Clemson College in South Carolina is dedicated to developing a mid-twentieth-century campus. Plate I is a view of the entire project in model form. In Plate II the building on the left shows the use of canopied overhangs to protect the window façade from the Southern sun, while the central part of the façade to the right in the photograph shows a variation on this theme in the projecting vertical columns. The buildings demonstrate the influence of component prefabricated window wall units on fenestration. (*Lyles, Bissett, Carlisle, and Wolff, Architects*)

*Plate II*

# IV. *Community and Institutional Buildings*

FOR the traditional South the church and the courthouse were far and away the most important—frequently the only—public and institutional buildings. Not only did they perform their special functions, but in those pre-movie, pre-TV days, a large part of the drama and recreation of the people centered in court day, the church social, the revival meeting. As industry, commerce, and the mass-entertainment business introduced such buildings as the factory, the railroad station, the office building, the store, the theater, and the stadium, these older institutions tended to become submerged in the new urban setting.

Let us look for a moment at the Southern church. While it is no longer completely dominant in the life of the people, it remains a most powerful influence, and in fact more recently there has been a great return to organized religion in the South. It is evidenced by the swelling building funds of the Protestant groups which are the dominating sects and by the new buildings of every kind of architecture and non-architecture. In architecture, the larger Protestant groups still tend to retain completely the eclectic neo-Georgian or Gothic shell and interior, with the benefits of modern technology for added comfort. However, some of the more progressive Protestant groups have shown themselves receptive to architectural change and have called upon the contemporary architects to help them try to attain a new aesthetic vitality comparable in force to that of the medieval Gothic. While a few good contemporary Protestant churches have been designed and built in the South, church architecture is changing from a religious emphasis to a community-center emphasis.

The Roman Catholic church with its powerful hierarchy and world-wide organization has always been keenly aware of the physical cravings and aesthetic appetites of its members and potential members. An appeal to the human being's basic sensuousness has always been used with adroitness by the Catholic church. This is one reason that Catholics throughout the history of Christianity have been great sponsors of the arts and architecture. The papal hierarchy recognized ten years or so ago the vitality of good contemporary architecture and issued an encyclical through its world organization encouraging its use.

For two thousand years (and even today in the democracies of the West) the Jews have been forced to adapt themselves to the new cultural climate of the dominant society. While they have maintained their independence and have remained sensitive to changing forms of architecture, most frequently their synagogues and temples have adopted a variation of the prevalent architectural forms. This is largely true in the South today.

City hall and courthouse remain the objects and symbols of civic pride in many of the smaller communities where the big buildings of industry and commerce are not present. But all too frequently, politics enters into the choice of designers for new buildings of this class, smothering all efforts at bold modern solutions. Contemporary architecture has its best chance when large-scale civic centers are being undertaken as part of overall urban redevelopment plans. New Orleans is a good example of such a happy circumstance, where the power of local government is expressing itself in a way reminiscent of the surge of community-center building in the United States in the 1920's.

While churches represent the older dominant type of institutional and public buildings (along with schools, which have been treated separately), hospitals and libraries are perhaps the characteristic buildings of contemporary culture at its best. Health is becoming a fetish with the American, and this is as true in the South as elsewhere. The Southern employee is beginning to look for all the fringe benefits which elsewhere result from employment in large organizations, whether in government or business. Counties are leaning toward building health organizations with central hospitals and outlying small hospitals and clinics. The concepts of preventive medicine are beginning to dominate the field, although the private practitioner still makes a handsome living from the middle classes who flock to his crowded office or small clinic.

The meaningful buildings in the health field which are making their appearance are the central hospital, the outpatient clinic, and the group medical clinic, with their supporting adjacent laboratories. Also, there is the chain hospital system operated by an industry or a union such as the United Mine Workers' chain in West Virginia and Kentucky.

Perhaps in no other type of building is the complete understanding of functional need and operation by the architect more necessary than in medical building design. An unfortunate development in this area is the entrance of the "hospital consultant," who is sometimes an architect and sometimes a hospital administrator. The architectural ideas of many of these consultants are ten years out of date before they reach the architect's program sheet, and by the time the hospital is designed and built they are fourteen years behind the times.

There is a glaring lack of understanding by hospital administrators and doctors, even in the university teaching hospitals, of the obligation of the medical profession to formulate a right and proper program for the function of a new medical building. Too often, questions of design get lost in squabbles, and the hospital may be built top-heavy in the area where the department head is most powerful, whether it has any relation to the community health needs or not. But, in spite of these hazards, some worthy hospitals have been built in the South in which careful attention was paid to proper programming of the health service needs of the region.

It is vital when undertaking a new hospital building program to work up a skelton staff complete with administrators and department heads who will work with the architect and the engineers concerned during the design and the construction of the building. When the hospital is completed, the entire design team can check it and then spend the time needed to give the new staff an understanding of the philosophy which generated the buildings, as well as to provide complete instruction in the operation and maintenance of all its complex machinery. A shipbuilder would not think of handing over a trans-Atlantic liner on her maiden voyage without first providing a thorough orientation period for the operating team. A modern hospital is no less complex. If the architect is to maintain his position as a master builder he must be more critical of the way in which he approaches the health building problem. Furthermore, the medical schools throughout the South should give graduate courses in conjunction with the architectural schools for hospital administrators and doctors who might become involved in building medical buildings.

The importance of the library in the community life of an educated society needs no emphasis. Although there are many architects who have done some creditable designs for new libraries, they work under the handicap that most librarians are extremely archaic in their outlook and in their resistance to new technology.

It is not only in the larger university and metropolitan library that a new philosophy should be developed. The small town and branch libraries are equally as vital to the life of a technologically oriented society. Such a library is an important link in the chain of continuing adult education. Libraries are no longer merely book repositories but are places which should be constantly giving courses to groups and encouraging individual study and self-improvement. Even small community libraries should, within the limits of their resources, inaugurate new cataloging systems and techniques in order to make themselves active rather than passive agents for community development.

Perhaps it could be argued that the most significant community building type in the modern South is the covered arena. In a society which glorifies the spectacle and at the same time places great emphasis on creature comforts, this building is a focus of community interest as a center of sports, religious revivals, and rock-and-roll festivals, to say nothing of the ice follies shows. At a time when people have immediate access to the world's top entertainers through TV, the theater and movie house have declined in importance in favor of the modern counterpart of the Roman Colosseum.

It is possible that the covered arena is replacing the football stadium as the dominant form in the world of sports and entertainment. It is true that the football stadium of the large university and the gigantic football arena, where the winning teams play off a national match, still hold an important place in the nostalgic yearnings of the alumni who wish to recapture their days spent at alma mater.

Large sums of money were invested in these outdoor structures through the 1930's and 1940's. Now, however, they may become a recessive in our culture. The ability to watch a scoring run by a football hero through the telephoto lens of the TV camera in the mechanically conditioned comfort of home or hotel room may become too much of a challenge to the stadium—just as it has to the movie house.

In the design of covered arenas the contemporary architect can legitimately show off his skill, a prowess which even the Romans with all their ingenuity could not approach. Such buildings can be covered by the use of steel in tension or by reinforced concrete in a structural shell form. Often the spans reach from two to three hundred feet across an arena which accommodates up to twelve thousand people, giving each person an uninterrupted view and still permitting as much as a two-hundred-foot free space for the spectacle. Architects have here a legitimate use for the constructivist approach, and some of the best examples of this type of building in the world are to be seen in the South. Too often, however, these magnificent buildings are located in an unplanned entourage of blighted and slum areas in which they are completely out of place.

An auditorium building is sometimes attached to one of these giant arenas in the present-day Southern city and is usually equipped with complete stage facilities for theatricals as well as for symphonies. Auditoriums are also included as part of the building complexes in large high schools, where they are often available for community use. Similarly, on university campuses they are to be seen in sizes ranging in audience capacity from five thousand down to five hundred.

In spite of TV, the modern Southern adult takes a healthy interest in continuing education and he supports all types of group programs. The contemporary architect has done a skillful and imaginative job in designing buildings which serve these programs and, in working closely with the engineer, has constantly improved the audial, visual, and physical comfort of the spectator.

This 270-foot-diameter coliseum for Georgia Institute of Technology in Atlanta is about one-third below ground level. In the below-surface part of the building the concrete bleachers are accommodated in an arena bowl literally scraped out of the earth after the steel-ribbed, semi-elliptical-shaped dome had been created. With its peripheral promenade at ground level inside the building, quick entrance and exit are guaranteed. The circular plan provides a flat, 132-foot-diameter, hard maple playing floor which is large enough for exhibition tennis including the backstop area or for two full-size basketball courts. (*Aeck Associates, Architects*)

The plastic form possible when reinforced concrete is used as a building material is well illustrated in the Henry Grady High School stadium in Atlanta, Georgia. The floodlight standards have been elegantly integrated into the simple structure of the stands. The cat ladder rungs have been cast into the back face of the standards, and the standards slope forward not only to bring the lights closer to

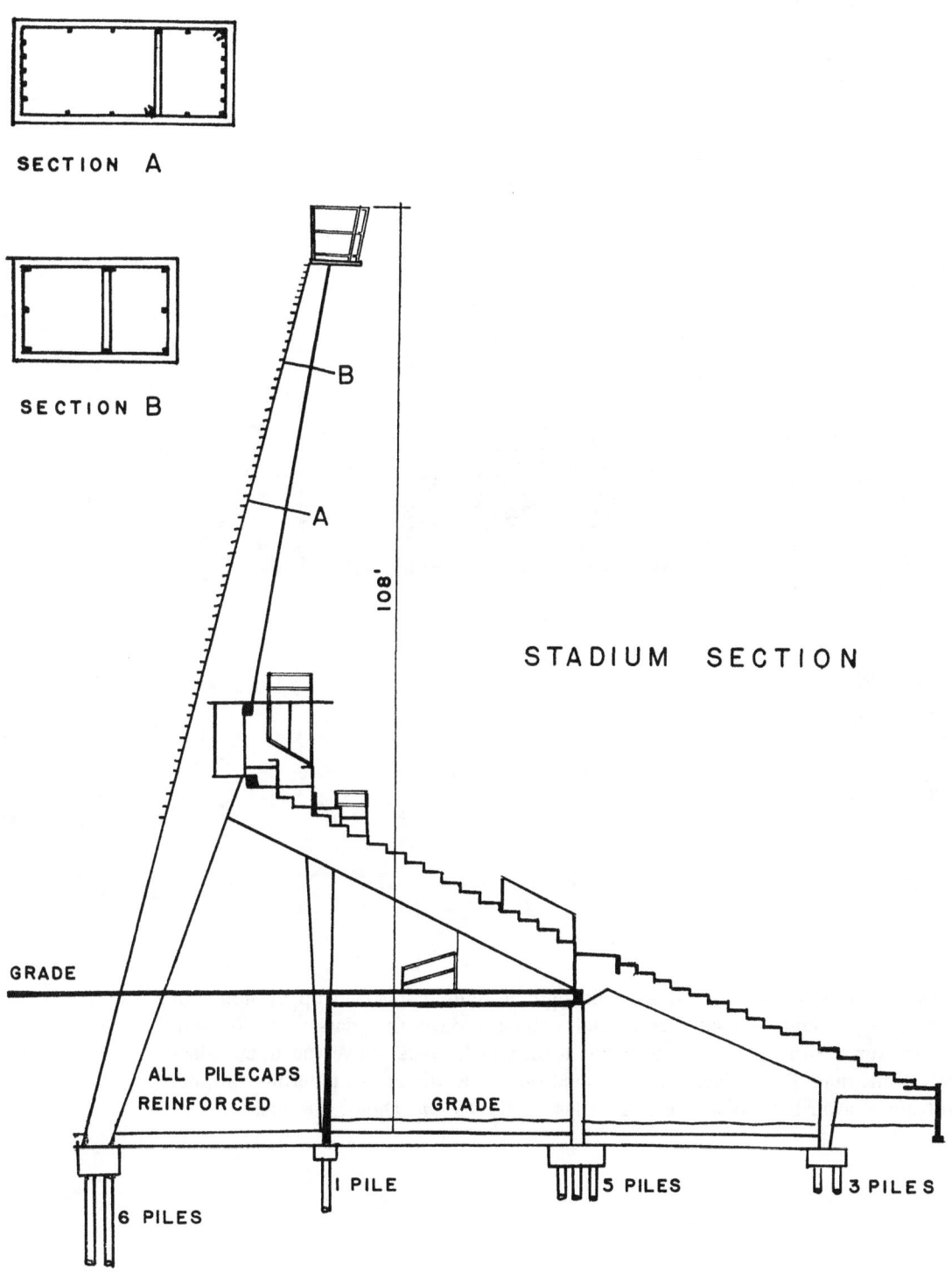

the playing field but also to make it easy for the electrician to climb the standard to the lighting platform. The designers located the stadium in such a way that it is entered from the rear at about the half-way level so that its cantilevered overhang forms a protected canopied foyer. The refreshment booths are located under the canopy. (*Aeck Associates, Architects*)

In this library, built in New Orleans, daylight is filtered into the upper floors of the building through pierced screen walls which protect the glass walls behind. This lacy surface forms a straightforward form which floats above the tinted glass panels of the main floor. Here is a fine solution and a winner of numerous national architectural awards for distinguished design. (*Curtis and Davis, Architects*)

This photograph shows a model for a proposed multi-story medical building for Atlanta, Georgia. It will be seen that automobiles can drive under the building, discharge their patients under cover, and then proceed to the parking deck in the rear. This design is included in this book because it shows clearly the influence of the mechanically controlled climate upon design. Such a solution is only feasible with year-round air-conditioning and good artificial lighting. In such a scheme the inner rooms of the building on each floor level have no windows, whereas the perimeter offices have small exterior windows which pierce the outer skin and are shielded from direct sun by vertical baffles. These baffles also serve as three-dimensional design elements in the treatment of the façades. The exterior sheathing walls are well insulated against summer heat and winter cold, and the building, which is square in plan, reduces heat loss and heat gain from outside temperatures to a minimum. Elevators and mechanical equipment are located in a central core. The philosophy of design expressed in this building is valid in this case; there is nevertheless danger that this type of thinking may become a formula, making architects careless about designing for natural climatic conditions and the natural physical environment. (*Edwards and Portman, Architects*)

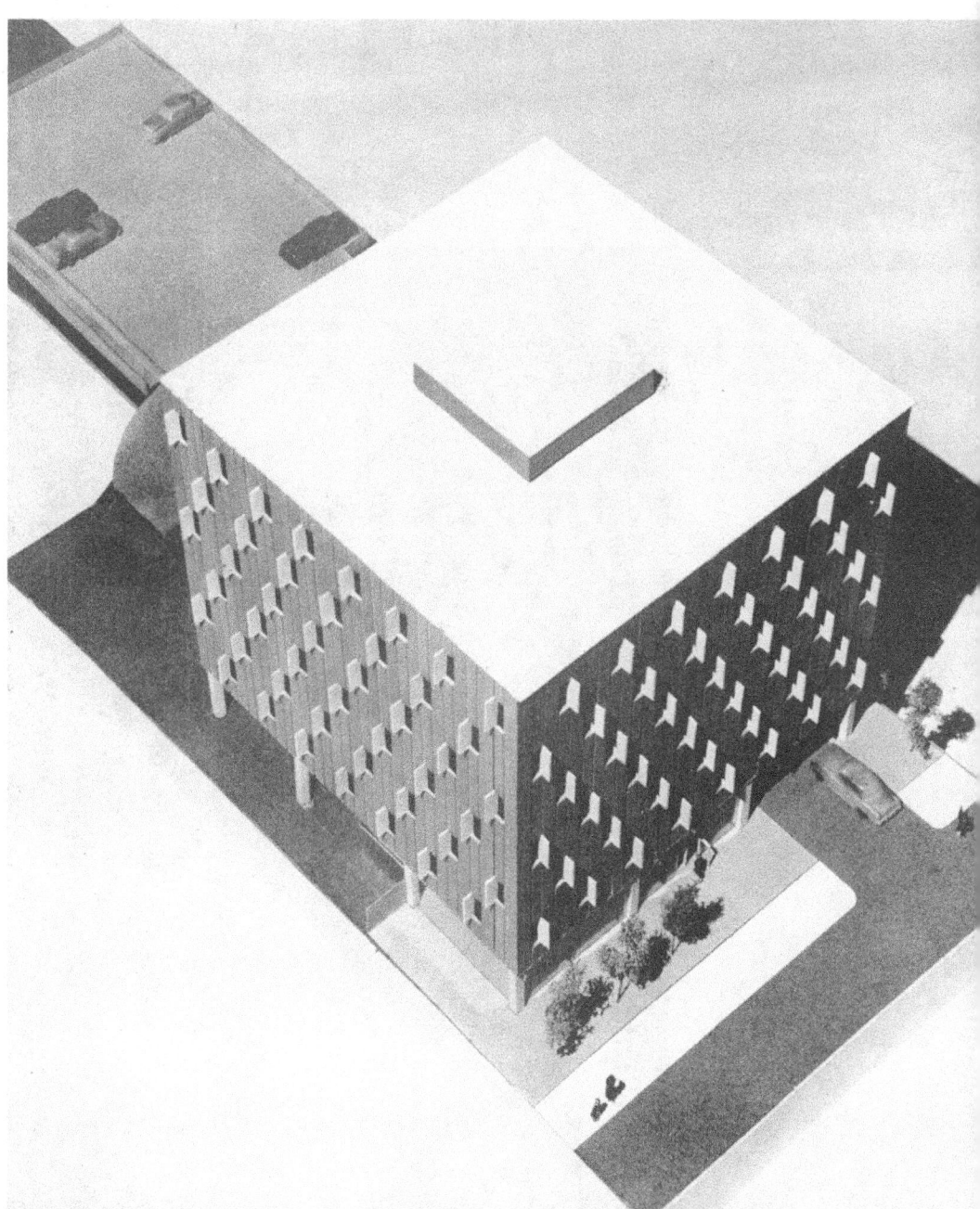

In this clean, straightforward library building, for the little town of Natchitoches, Louisiana, the detailing and general concept are based on the structural formalism of steel-column bays connected with beams and an integration of the glass sheath into the rhythm of the design. Almost Grecian simplicity has been maintained by floating the floor of the building above the ground. This device differs from that of the Greeks only in that they did not have steel but carried their building freely above the ground on a flat stone stylobate. The building introduces a welcome change of rhythm in the glass walls by the use of floor-to-ceiling operating jalousies. This gives the building a subtle feeling of hot-climate design without belaboring the point. (*Barron, Heinberg and Brocato, Architects*)

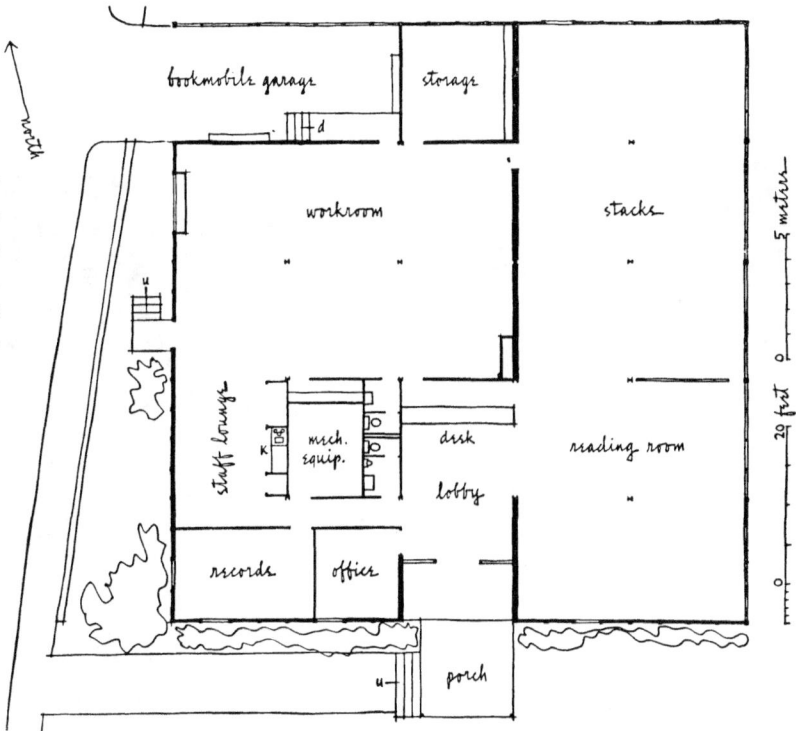

*Plate I*

The Harlan Memorial Hospital of the Miners Memorial Hospital Association in Harlan, Kentucky, is one of a chain of ten hospitals built in a 250-mile strip of country located on the border of Kentucky, West Virginia, and Virginia. Here is an example of team design in which skilled hospital administrators worked closely with architects and engineers to design a regional system of hospitals, complete down to a common

*Plate II*

teletype bookkeeping system. The working core of this well-organized hospital is the various specialized medical, surgical, and pharmaceutical facilities which are readily related to the nursing wards and outpatient areas. The first floor (Plate IV) of the Harlan Hospital has the specialized laboratories and the surgical suite in a line along a connecting corridor. On the other side of this corridor are the outpatient facilities (flanked by the outpatient waiting lobby), with the central records and admitting office adjoining them in the center of the building. The main elevators to the hospital above are also centrally located. The storeroom for hospital supplies completes the space use of this floor. Its location is one of the best features of the hospital plan, since one dispatcher can make up the daily orders for each nursing station and deliver them (packed on mobile supply carts) by way of the special elevator. The carts are delivered during the night hours to reduce congestion in the corridors. A full cart is exchanged for an empty one, and any supplies with unbroken seals are returned to the stores. Hospital supply accounting is simplified, because charts for drugs can be passed straight from the supply store to central records across the hall and the nurses are thus relieved of accounting problems. Furthermore, the pharmacy can draw its supply readily from the same source. In Plate IV it may be seen that the emergency entrance gives direct access to surgery, with good control from central records and admittance. Similarly,

*Plate III*

outpatient control desks (Plate III) are placed close to central records, the hub of the hospital. Surgery is also well placed for drawing supplies and for using the laboratory facilities. (*Sherlock, Smith and Adams, Architects*)

*Plate IV*

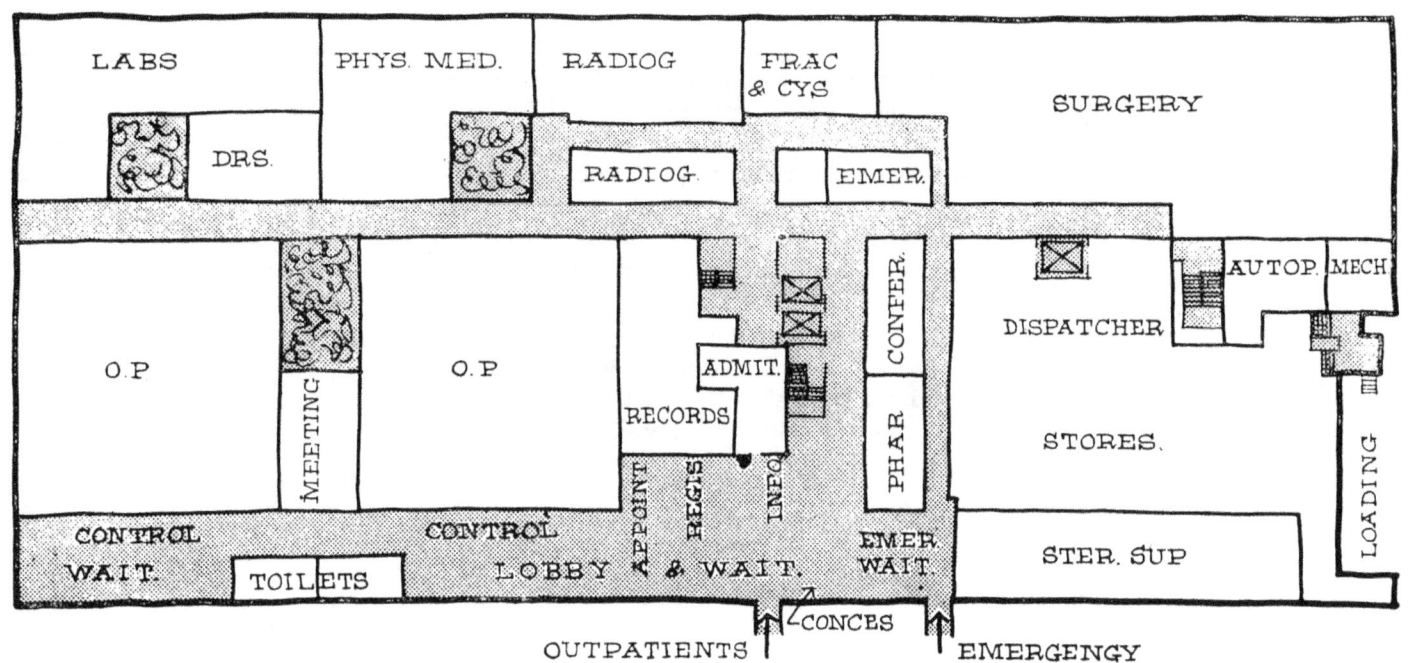

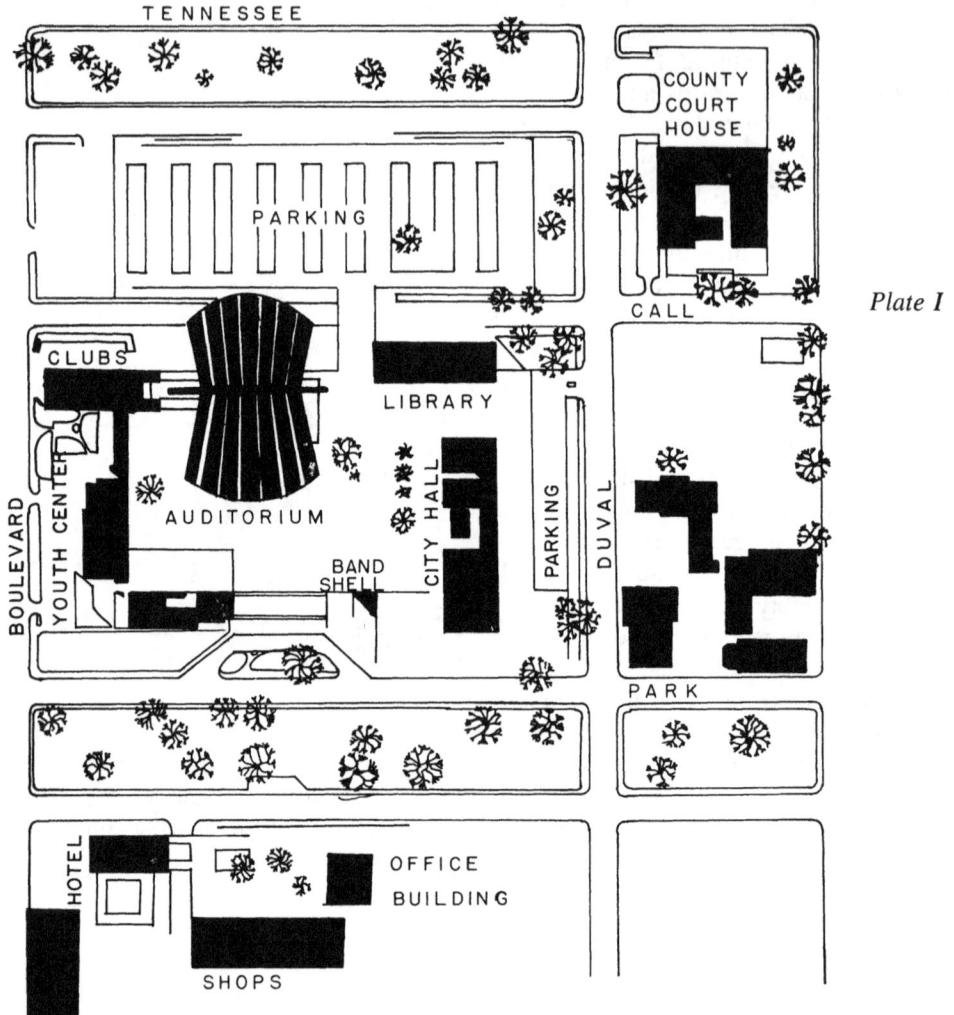

Plate I

Tallahassee, Florida, is a city of less than fifty thousand population with great and worthy ambitions. This is well illustrated by the comprehensive civic center which is being designed for this community. One can see in Plate I the large auditorium which becomes the focal center of a paved and landscaped super block. At first only the auditorium was contemplated; it would have been situated in a blighted and crowded area. The architects suggested integrating this main structure into a whole complex of needed civic buildings complete with office buildings, band shell, city hall, and parking facilities. They also suggested, by way of helping the city reduce the financial burden of building several kinds of auditoriums, a multi-purpose structure. The planning of the spaces between the buildings has been as carefully done as the buildings themselves. No automobile will be allowed in the plaza, which was designed to include shade trees and a lagoon. The highly flexible circular center of the auditorium building may be cleared for banquets, skating, and dancing; it may be filled with seats for any kind of exhibition from little theater to basketball. There are no structural members to obstruct the view, and a bank of 3,375 fixed seats surround this space. The asymmetrical fans of the remainder of the building may be divided for spectator seating. For the larger events a double deck of sheltered parking has been provided for a thousand cars. In Plate II a model of the auditorium is shown. The folded-plate, rhythmical half cylinders are supported in the center by a parabolic arch while they fan out at the extremities to be supported by columns. Although this building provides great flexibility of use for all types of gatherings, it is obvious that the architects must have been strongly influenced by Le Corbusier's *Palais des Soviets à Moscou, 1931*. (Architects Collaborative, Architects)

Plate II

The new courthouse in Montgomery, Alabama beautifully demonstrates that municipal architecture does not have to remain under the dead hand of traditionalism. The structure of the inner court, although rather heavily modulated, is a product of the better architectural thinking of the day. (*Pearson, Tittle, and Narrows, Architects*)

This Winston-Salem, North Carolina, coliseum uses a technique well known to the ancient Greeks, that of dropping the arena seating into the ground, thus making it possible for the public to enter at ground level and go down to half of the amphitheater seats and up to the other half. The 210-foot-span steel arches are made up as straight segments welded together. The arches were delivered to the job in two-segment lengths, and the cranes which erected them operated from ground level, thus saving a tremendous cost in erection time and necessary rigging. The horizontal thrust of these arches is taken by steel used in tension, and these tie-rods are suspended on one-inch-diameter rods from the arches. The building is a good example of how an architectural and engineering team can work to overcome the skyrocketing cost of both shop and field erection of structural steel. This is probably the most economical structure of its kind built in the mid-twentieth century in the United States. In this building the roof literally went on first. Then the excavation was made to complete the concrete bleachers, all under cover from the weather. The building has 168 feet of exit doorway around its perimeter so that a crowd of ten thousand can completely evacuate the building in four minutes. (*Edward W. Waugh and G. Milton Small, Architects*)

*Plate 1*

Charlotte, North Carolina, is a city of some 150,000 people, who voted a $4,700,000 bond issue to provide the city with a large athletic, cultural, and exhibit center. The three main elements in the design of this group, to be placed on a 23 acre site, were a coliseum, an auditorium, and later, an exhibition hall. The design problem was extremely difficult, because a 13,500-seat coliseum had to be related to a much smaller auditorium so that the two buildings would be successful as a related

*Plate II*

complex without the presence of the third or exhibition building which would complete the group later. The architects solved this problem by spacing the two buildings two hundred feet apart and using the space between as a tree-planted concourse with a slender, covered walk connecting them. The designers are to be congratulated, because they have kept all parking away from the environs of the

Plate III

building and provided for a good tree-planting program which will be in the tradition of the planting of the preceeding two centuries in the South. The massive parking lots have been located across streets from the main site and others will be added as land is made available. This makes possible the quick emptying of the parking lots into the surrounding traffic arteries. The interior of the coliseum shows how

*Plate IV*

the combined genius of designer and structural engineer can create a vast arena by using lattice-work steel structure in the form of a spherical cap. Plate IV of the building under construction shows how light these lattice ribs are; the heavier ring in the center is a compression ring and has cartwheel spokes to help resist the crushing load, both live and dead. The exterior, horizontal thrust of

Plate V

the dome is taken up by the exterior steel tension ring which is supported by the rhythmically placed steel columns. They are covered with concrete to afford fire protection for the steel. The building fits American production technology in the repetitive use of prefabricated members which form the lattice work of the

Plate VI

vast dome. This 330-foot roof span has a remarkably light weight per square foot. In the lounge (Plate V) the architect's collaborators have created an abstract mural which ties the back wall and the sloping ceiling together, providing a light, transparent emphasis for an area which might otherwise be gloomy. The

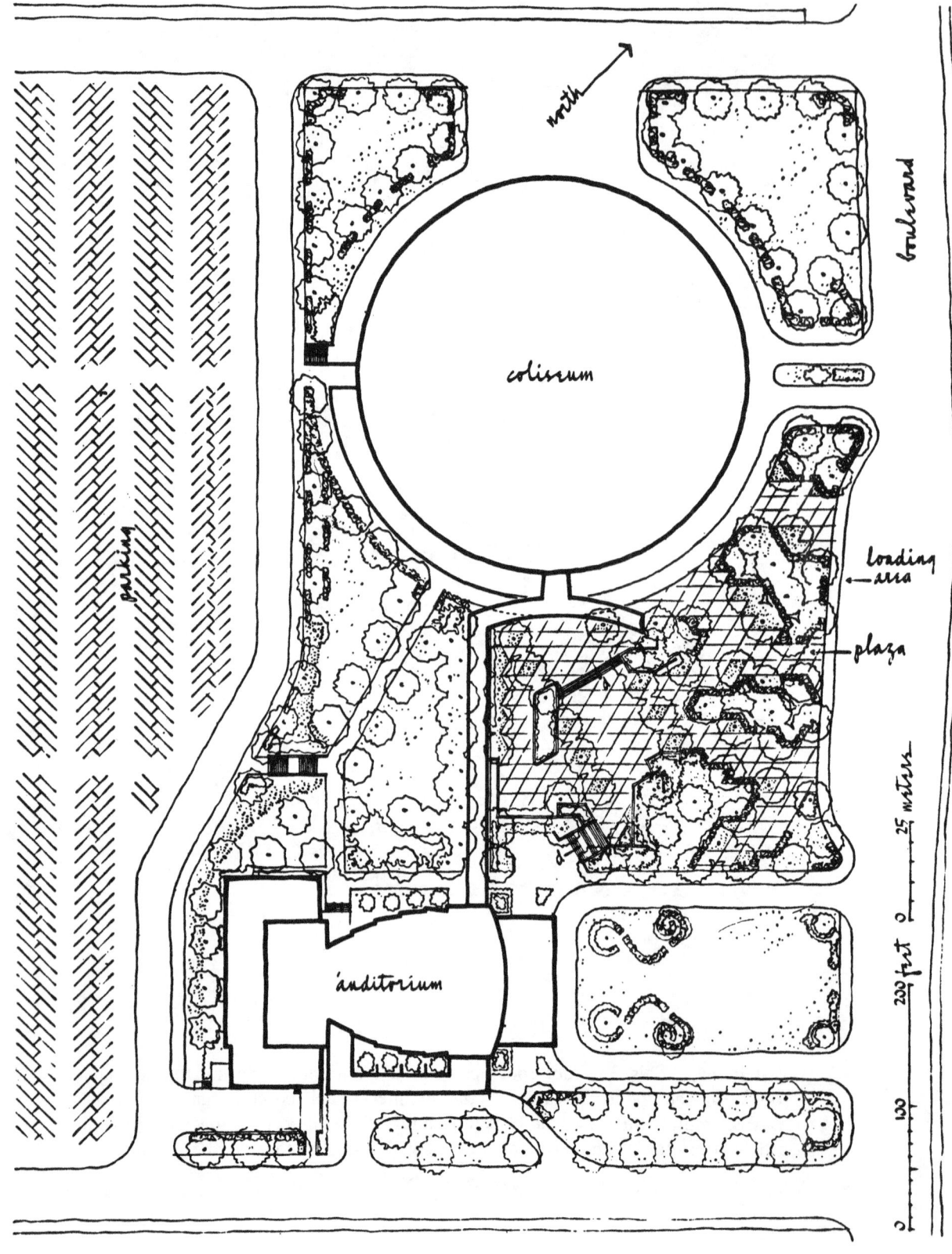

Plate VII

stairs (Plate VI) maintain this lightness by appearing almost afloat in space when silhouetted against the glass walls of the lobby. (*A. G. Odell, Jr., and Associates, Architects*)

*Plate I*

This Louisiana church has the simple dignity of a tented canopy. The rippling edges of the folded-plate canopied roof are gathered together in one ridge line down the center of the nave. This roof form is a precise, contemporary abstraction of the Gothic lancet vaults of the thirteenth century which were then built of stone. However, in the case of Gothic architecture the vault rhythm was seen only from within, as the upper surface had to be covered to make it waterproof. Modern building technology skillfully used by the designers here has enabled them to produce a light, refined structure. Daylight has been introduced along the edge of

Plate III

the roof and reflected up to the ceiling so that the whole canopy is washed with even illumination by day and by indirect lighting at night. The recessed circular lights at night give a spotted brilliance to the roof canopy. The wood screen at the east of the church defines the sanctuary and seems to enfold the altar within it. From the exterior west-end view a highly textured masonry wall connects a free-standing cross to the main body of the church to give a dramatic impact. (*Curtis and Davis, Architects*)

Plate II

95

Plate I

This nurses' home and school was constructed in Bristol, Tennessee, to accommodate thirty-two student nurses and provide living quarters for two supervisors and a small group of graduate nurses. The foundations, floors, roof, and framing are all of concrete and the walls are of brick and concrete block. The interior partitions are variously of concrete block, metal, and brick. The building was designed so that a third floor might be added. At present all student rooms are located on the outside walls of the second floor (Plate III) and laundry, lounges, toilets, kitchen, and stairs form the core of this floor. Among other features which identify the building as well designed and comfortable are the steel skeletal frame and the glass window walls modulated by solid brick curtain walls at the ends. (*A. L. Aydelott and Associates, Architects*)

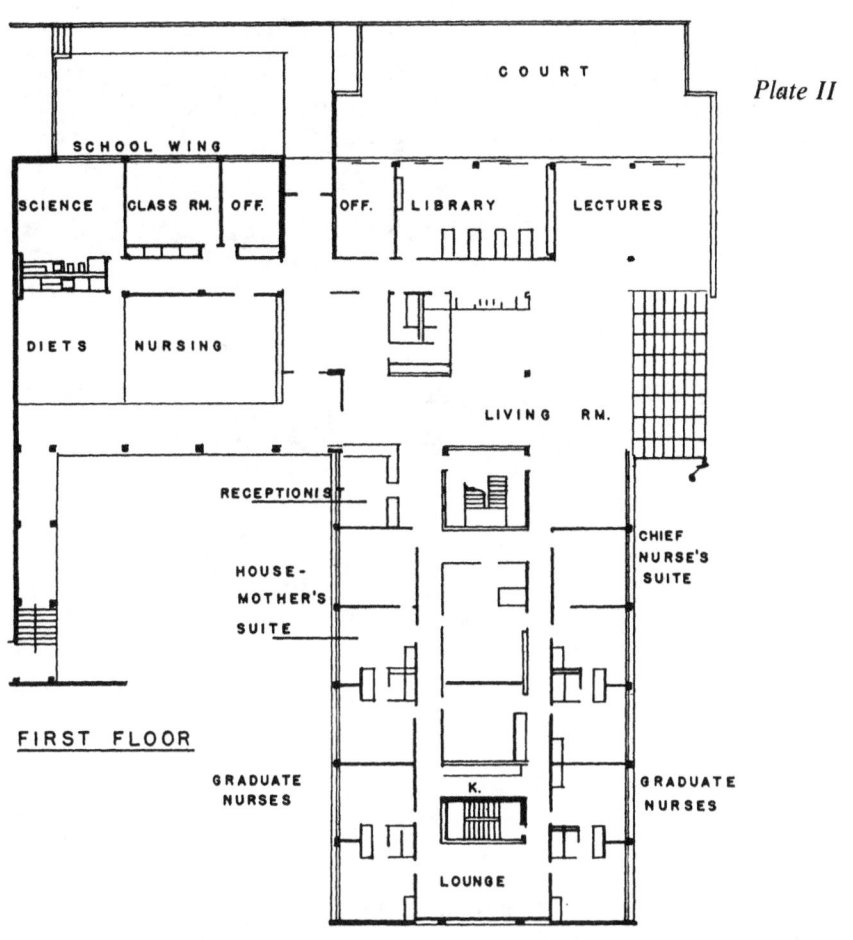

*Plate II*

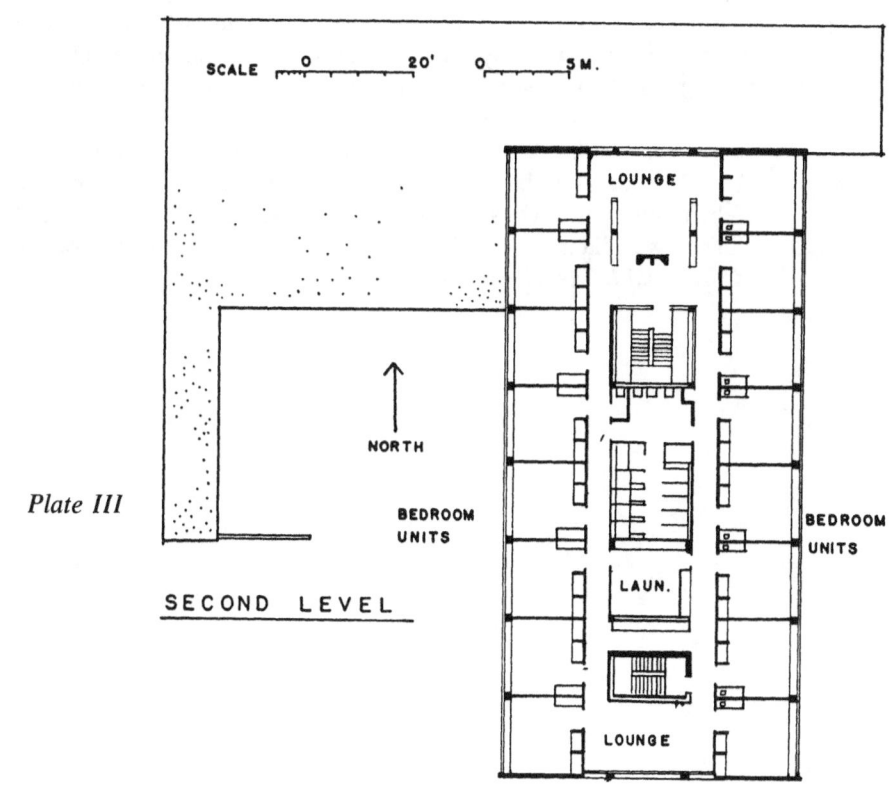

*Plate III*

Plate I

Bayou LaFourche, a rural community in the extreme south of Louisiana near a main highway, is the site of this pediatric clinic. Because the area is swampy and subject to flooding by hurricanes, the building is raised above the ground. Square terra-cotta flue tile is used on the main façade as a sun screen in front of the glass walls. This treatment creates a definite, refined rhythm of alternating blank and solid. The entrance is a covered walk in front of a well-landscaped patio. An inner patio is divided by an inside glass wall from the main waiting room. This patio gives an open spaciousness to the interior of the building and allows daylight to penetrate some of the interior. The covered walkway which wraps around the end of the building from the main entrance encloses a second patio (Plates I and II). The total building has a simple rectangular form, but because of the method of handling these patios the interior achieves greater interest and variation. The clinic is well planned for a heavy load of outpatients in addition to a few inpatients. (*Curtis and Davis, Architects*)

Plate III

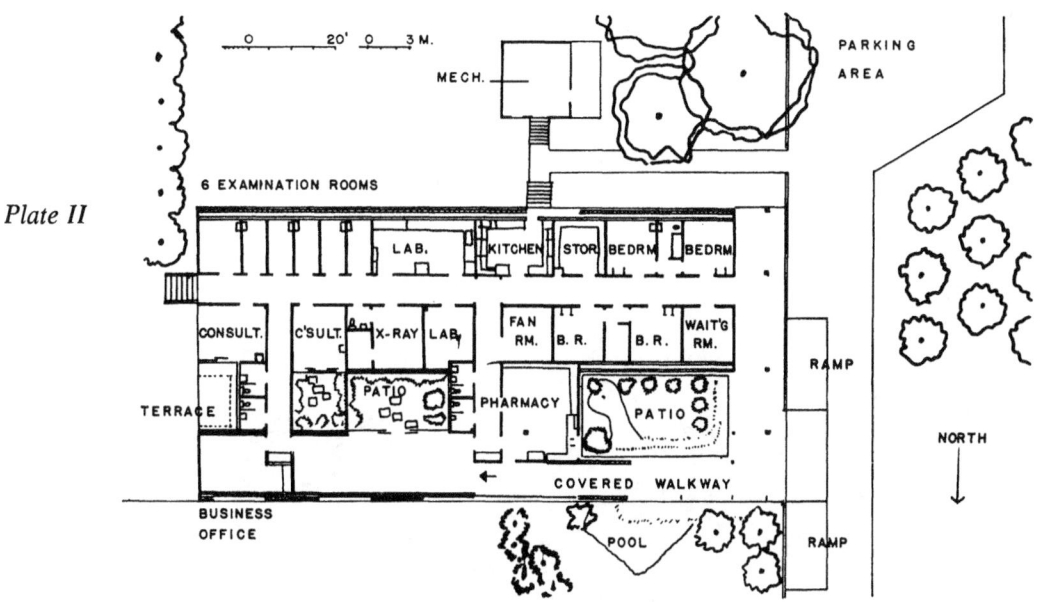

*Plate II*

*Plate I*

In this Lutheran church in Conover, North Carolina, pointed arch frames of laminated wood have been used, covered with wood roof deck and with standing-seam copper roofing as the waterproofing medium. The entrance (Plate I) has a rather flat arch, while the arch at the sanctuary end has a shorter base and an acute point of much greater altitude (Plate II) resulting in a sloping ridge line. The intervening arches, which are equally spaced between the two extremes, not only come progressively closer together at their bases as they approach the sanctuary but rise in height along the ridge line. This treatment dramatizes the sanctuary by causing the roof space to soar upward from the comparatively low entrance (Plate I) to the sanctuary end (Plates II and III). The structuring here also produces a gracefully compounded curve in the roof surface. This type of curve is known to geometricians as a linear curve. Constructivist sculpture has been greatly influenced in creation of its forms by this type of space geometry. In turn, it has influenced contemporary architecture. Although the sanctuary is the most significant part of this design, there is also interest in the way in which the Sunday-school and assembly rooms are grouped (Plate IV) to form a quadrangle to the right of the sanctuary. (*A. G. Odell, Jr., and Associates, Architects*)

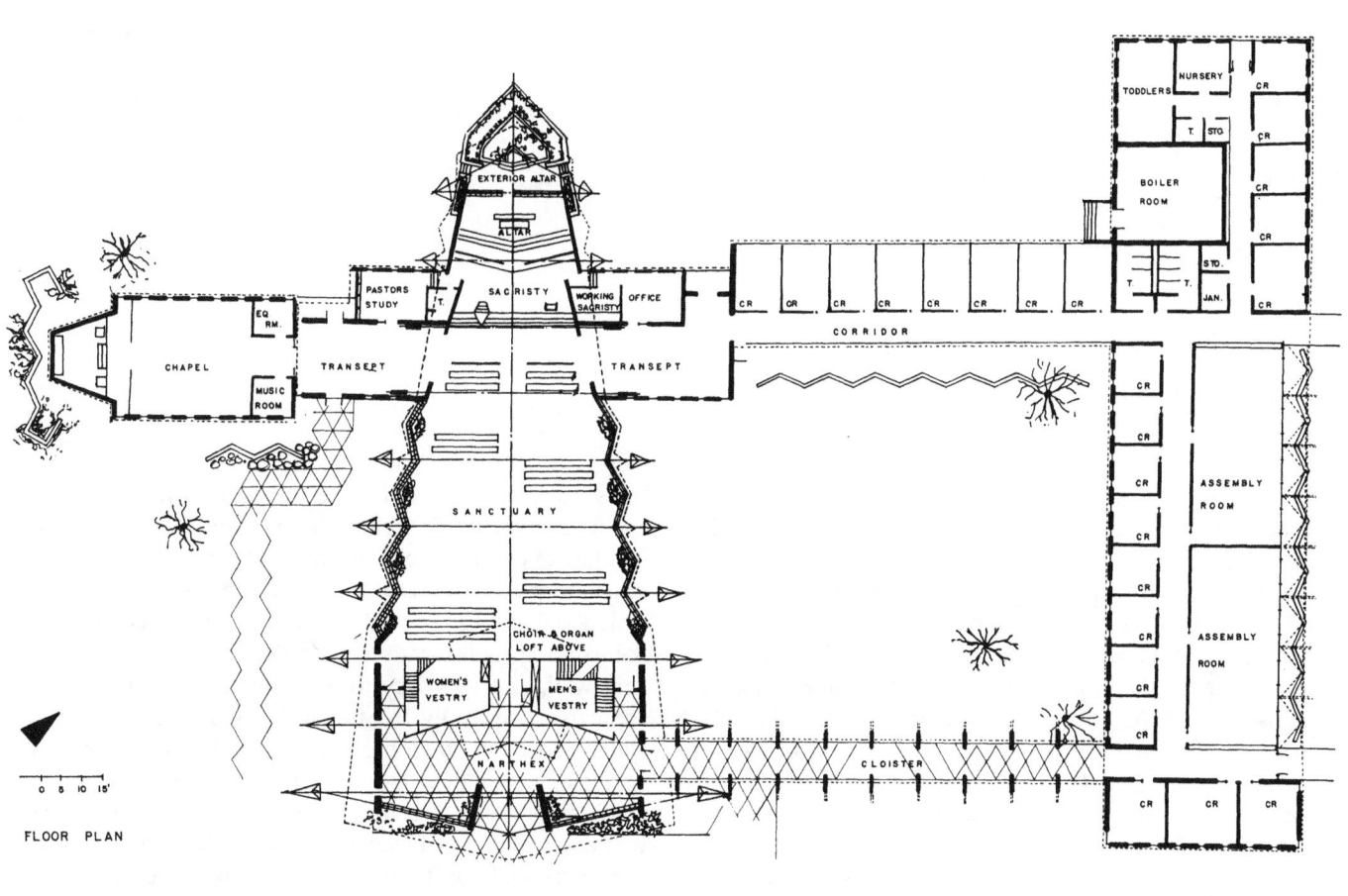

Plate III

Plate IV

Plate I

The Livestock Judging Pavilion in Raleigh, North Carolina, designed for the North Carolina State Fair, is the result of a collaborative effort between William H. Deitrick, Raleigh architect, and design consultant Matthew Nowicki, with Severud-Elsted-Krueger as engineers. William Deitrick was responsible for the execution of the working drawings and supervision of construction after the death of Matthew Nowicki, who created the original design. In the few years which have elapsed since the construction of this building, it has become internationally known among architects and informed laymen because of its significant architectural form. The structural system was developed to span a large space in an economical manner. High-quality steel cables were strung in catenary form between two scissored, opposing arches. The roof loads place the cables in tension in the plane of the arches, and the load is thus translated into compression which is carried down the concrete arches to the ground. The window mullions are actually necessary to the support of the dead weight of the arches. They also form a skeleton to which the glass is attached; of course the mullions have to resist horizontal wind loads on the glass walls. The designers made ingenious use of these mullions to support the wood forms used when the reinforced concrete arches were being poured into place. The buried ends of the arches are tied together with prestressed steel cables placed in an underground tunnel. The ends of the roof cables are attached to the arches by tension springs which provide the flexibility needed to accommodate the roof surface to varying degrees of uplift created by wind motion overhead. In Plate II one may see that the majority of the bleacher seats are placed opposite the center line of the building, which is ideal for spectator sports. From the interior the exciting shell form seems to float above the translucent wall, and it is easy to see why architectural critics are carried away by the building. However, the glass walls make the building unsuitable for any kind of performance which requires artificial lighting during daylight hours. A solution of the acoustical problem was one which was faced at the outset but not included in the original construction contracts because of budget problems. It was, however, solved with some ingenuity by suspending fibre board baffles from the steel roof cables to make a textured pattern (Plate II). This was done after the building had been completed and had proved to be acoustically untenable. Plate III is one of Nowicki's original design sketches. As a structure this building might be called a supported steel shell in which the interwoven cables support the light-gauge, pre-formed roof deck. This kind of structure, in which the stresses are taken in the tension cables, seems much more suitable to American production techniques than a compression concrete shell might be, because this type of building needs no molding into shape by expensive, temporary form work. (*William H. Deitrick, Architect, Matthew Nowicki, Design Consultant, and Severud-Elsted-Krueger, Engineers*)

*Plate II*

*Plate III*

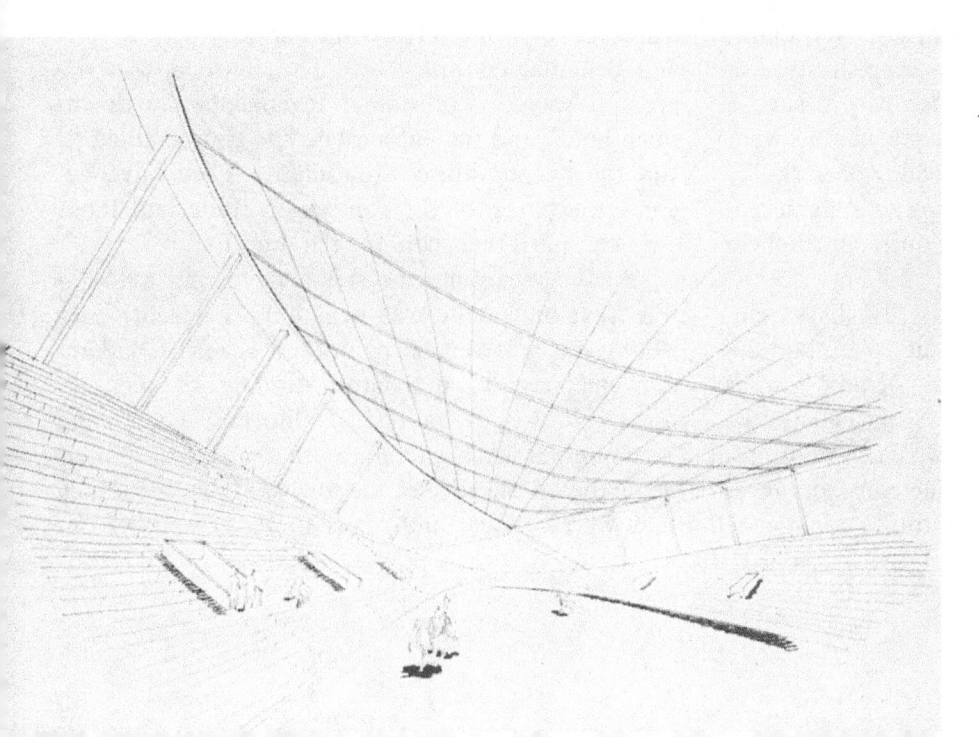

# V. Commercial and Industrial Buildings

JUST as the cathedral with its towering spire was designed to dominate the medieval city, so the skyscraper office building was designed to show the power of the modern corporate organization which it represents. From the time of Louis Sullivan to World War II it could be fairly said that the skyscraper was the dominant architectural symbol of our urban civilization. Today that is no longer true. The skyscraper took its form in the period of rail transportation and the intense development of the central cores of our cities which grew out of it. But all through the twentieth century the automobile has been gaining in its rivalry with the railroad as a means of human and freight transportation, and in the period since World War II its complete victory can be seen in the city's blitzkrieg invasion of the surrounding countryside. The suburban shopping center, the motel, the airport, the factory in the fields—all of these are rivaling the skyscraper as significant architectural forms of the day.

The modern shopping center has developed during the past decade into a complex of commercial buildings reflecting nearly every aspect of modern living. Located on the outskirts of the city, it reproduces all the features of the downtown shopping area in a setting which is designed to cater entirely to the automobile customer. The idea started in the 1920's with the Kansas City Plaza. Although it was built in the neo-Spanish style, it was beautifully executed and landscaped in such a manner that automobiles were hidden behind well-placed shrub walls and trees. A feeling of park-like penetration of the building groups was achieved, and about the whole there was a quiet atmosphere for shopping.

In the immediate post-war years, English architects, with their long tradition of city planning, developed the shopping mall. This carried the Kansas City idea a step further to the point where the pedestrian could move about freely and safely in a landscaped central mall with double entrance stores and shops surrounding it, one entrance facing the mall, the other facing the parking area on the periphery.

It is most regrettable that from such auspicious beginnings the modern shopping center has deteriorated into a series of island blocks on which are concentrated the various stores surrounded by seas of asphalt. The poorly controlled automobile drivers vie with each other for the ever-lessening number of parking spaces. The wretched pedestrian is confined to one of the island blocks unless he is willing to take life in hand and not only cross a mass of parked automobiles but also several lanes of moving traffic. In view of the tremendous amount of skill which has been expended by architect-planners in developing the mall shopping center as an over-all design providing segregation of pedestrian and automobile traffic and maintaining a quiet atmosphere, it is a sad commentary on our society that so many new shopping centers in the South are abuilding at this moment which show complete disregard for the sound principles that have been evolved.

In the roaring 1920's the skyscraper hotel appeared all over the nation, including the South. Usually it was a great brick pile with carefully spaced windows for the rooms. Up near the fifteenth floor the remnant of our Georgian past was displayed in white terra cotta cornices with dentils and ornamented brackets. The railroad was the greatest source of customer revenue to the downtown hotel, and the automobile has almost killed it. But the twenty stories still stand. They have become the haven of the convention trade and those who can park their cars for the duration.

In the meantime the steadily growing automobile-traveling public was beginning to resent, after a long day's drive, the pomp and splendor and inconvenience and mandatory tipping of the city hotel. It was probably in California, where land was not yet at a premium, that the first motels appeared on the edge of the towns. In their infancy they were cheaper and easier to get in and get out of than hotels, and tipping was forbidden. It did not take long, however, for the small business speculator to find out that the deluxe motel, where people could still park free, would be in even greater demand than the cheaper motel. Then came the motel chains. Today, every Southern town boasts at least one first-class air-conditioned motel, complete with restaurant, swimming pool, and with an essay at some landscaping. The population push is unfortunately already beginning to bring about the two-story motel and the six-story counterpart, the downtown motor hotel. Again, diminishing returns in economical hostelry can be foreseen.

The airport has become one of the most important and specialized buildings of the larger Southern city today. Architecturally it should be the open portal which receives passengers and freight from the air for disbursement on land. Constructivism finds a genuine use in such a building, and even the humanist architect might legitimately become a formalist. The integration of the control tower, fundamental to the airport as its command post, into the whole complex of automotive approaches, parking areas, shops, restaurants, not to speak of the essential areas for loading, unloading, and servicing the planes themselves, becomes the problem of designing a city within the city and should be undertaken only by the architect with city planning background.

While the bus station is part of the twentieth-century city, in significance it takes a secondary position to the airport. Usually located in a downtown area, it does not have to be a city within the city. When well conceived architecturally, the bus station becomes a kind of contemporary version of the nineteenth-century rail terminal. The new ones in the South are usually done in the modern architectural idiom, some good, some inexcusable.

As in the design of the airport, a place where the formalist architect who follows the structural synthesis approach really comes into his own is in the design of the modern factory building. Here the column-and-beam spacing, interspersed with electrically operated and electronically controlled production machinery, almost demands an architectural environment of repetitive modules of continuous window walls with heat-controlling glass, of modulated skyline bubbles on the roof. Played up against this simple rectangular structure, the administrative offices are often set apart in a dignified two-story building with benefit of Brazilian architect Niemeyer's brise-soleil. An important and dominating feature of the executive office grouping is often the brilliant interplay of interior and exterior spaces and courts and the use of well-conceived landscaping and big planting.

Television studios and stations are beginning to appear as part of the entourage of even the small Southern city. So far this particular medium is in its infancy, and perhaps it is too early to predict the evolving architectural form, although some early examples follow closely along the pattern of the small industrial factory with the very simple studio area (not unlike a rectangular barn) and nearby the executive offices and program control center. This latter area is usually in a separate and richer kind of building. Of course the most dominating element of the TV station is the steel microwave tower which is usually outside the city limits—at least the present limits.

A new and vivid architecture has appeared in the South in the structural design which has grown from chemical engineering. Its forms are the direct expression of the production processes required. There is nothing which more clearly epitomizes the mid-twentieth century than the giant petroleum cracking plant or the synthetic rubber plant. While few of these plants have had the benefit of architectural service, except the office buildings, the engineers translate the functional requirements so honestly (as they have in the construction of great bridges) that the forms more often than not turn out to be good design. Another building type which exhibits an exciting form, this time in poured reinforced concrete, is the great grain elevator. It can be seen disgorging its gigantic volume capacity into the holds of ships in every Southern seaport, particularly in the Gulf Coast cities.

The modern architect cannot avoid a war that is now underway as a result of the spreading of the city over the countryside. A part of this war is the battle between the downtown merchants and the merchants of the outer shopping centers. A tremendous amount of money has been invested by leading banks and insurance companies in downtown buildings, as it has in town factories, which are also showing a tendency to migrate outside of city limits. The money-controlling institutions are obviously not going to abandon their heavy capital investment, and the fight to save the original downtown is coming more and more into the open. The kind of redevelopment that the Mellon fortune promoted in Pittsburgh may be necessary to save many of our Southern cities. The new Civic Center development in New Orleans is a short step in this direction.

It is quite clear that there is going to be a long struggle between the desire of the average city dweller and shopper to escape from the concrete wilderness of the downtown metropolis and the desire of the investor to protect his enormous investment. If the Southern architect, either the one in practice or the fledgling about to leave the architectural school, does not assume the responsibility and the social obligation imposed upon an ancient and respected profession to join in this fight and help to bring it to a proper conclusion, then American cities in the new South will be left to the arbitrary control of the speculator, the highway engineer, the layman boards, the planner who is not an architect. In this respect architects are already shamefully tardy. To state it simply, modern architecture and modern architects have no great significance unless they accept responsibility for over-all city and regional planning.

The architects of Rich's Department Store in Knoxville, Tennessee, have shown that the modern problem of this type of operation may be most successfully solved when handled by a first-rate design team. The site plan and schematic section in Plate IV show the horizontal circulation of the building complex as well as the vertical relationships of the circulation. Here two adjacent city blocks have been developed from the high ground on Locust Street to the low ground of the second block to the west. The architects have fronted the department store on Locust to pick up the important pedestrian traffic of a large city center, while they have provided parking decks in the second building which connects with the main store by an underground ramp. It will also be seen that deliveries are made on this level from

the warehouse, and the customer may pick up household items from the bargain basement on his way to his automobile parked in the rear. The receiving department is one floor below and enables all trailer trucks to come in at this level without becoming involved with local deliveries or customers' cars. It is good to see a large department store permit the use of land for planting and ornamental pools. One feels certain, as the trees grow, that there will be some return to the elegance of the era of shade trees. (*Stevens and Wilkinson, Architects, in collaboration with Raymond Loewy and Associates and Eckbo, Royston, and Williams as landscape designers*)

3RD
2ND
LOCUST STREET
LOCUST ST. LEVEL
HENLEY ST. LEVEL
SERVICE AREA
HENLEY STREET
SERVICE TUNNEL
CUSTOMER PICK-UP
PARKING DECKS
DELIVERIES
RECEIVING
CHURCH ST. LEVEL
CLINCH ST. LEVEL
N
CHURCH AVENUE
LOCUST STREET
STORE
HENLEY STREET
WAREHOUSE
MERCHANDISE DELIVERY
RECEIVING DOCK
CUSTOMER PICK-UP
CUSTOMER PARKING
CHUTE
FREIGHT ELEVATOR
CLINCH AVENUE

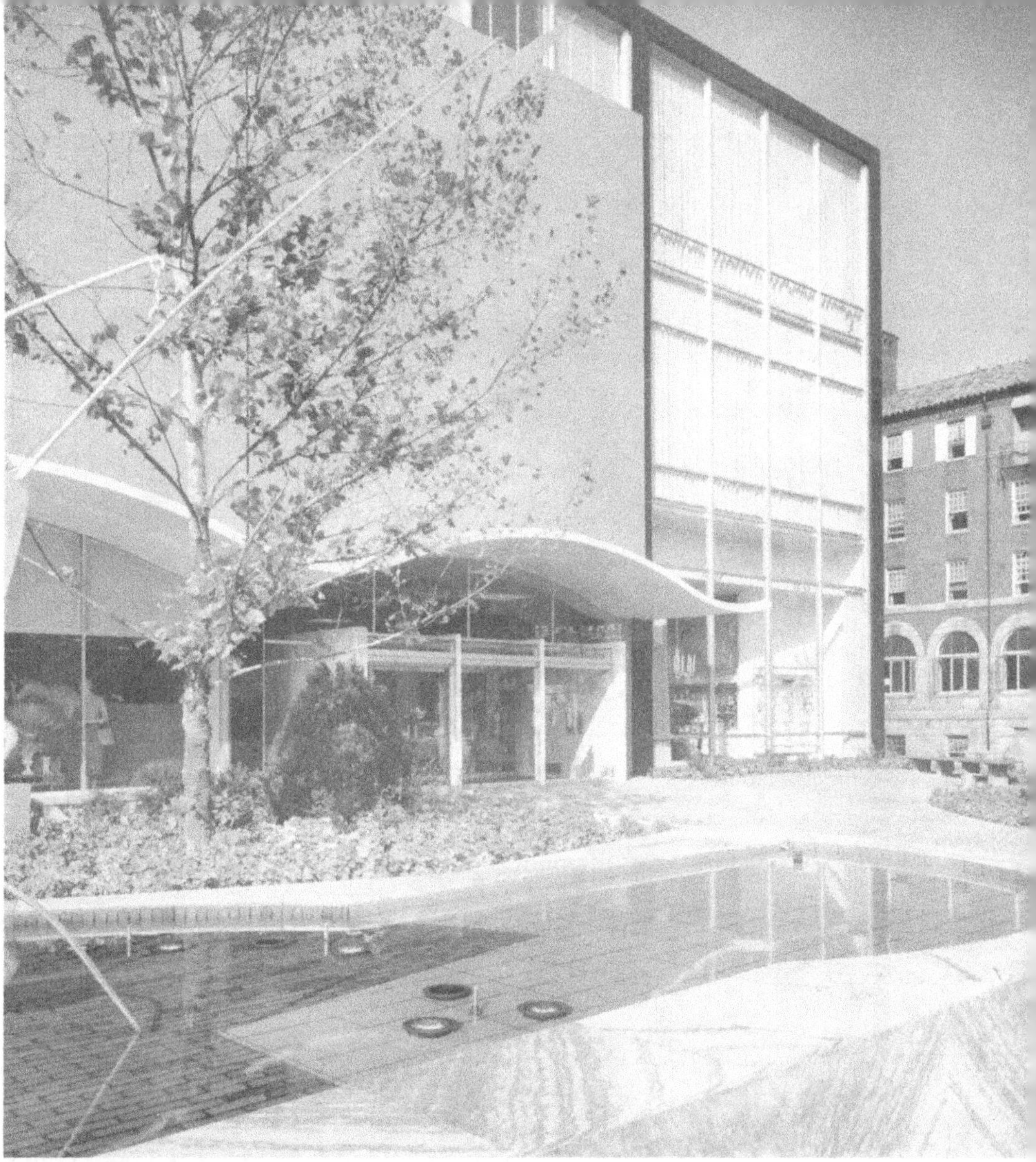

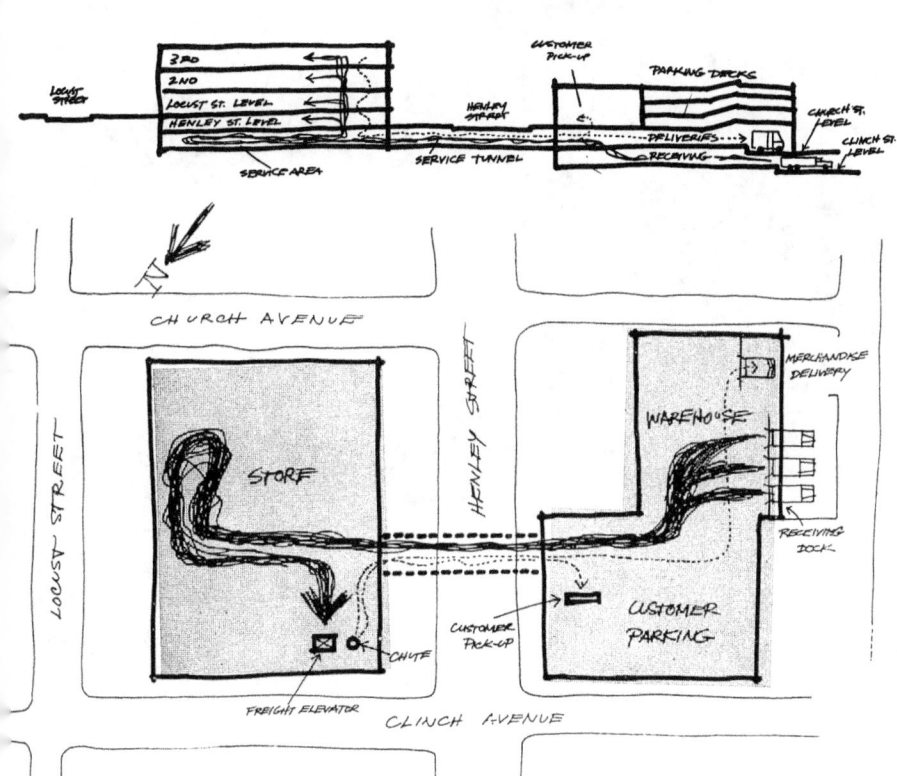

Plate II

Because of its long standing position as the major seaport of the Gulf of Mexico, New Orleans has always been influenced by what goes on in that area as well as South America. In the Carib Building this influence is seen. The play of light and shade in the leaf pattern on the sidewalk and lower screen walls here has been picked up in the design of the brise-soleil of the upper three floors. This subtlety gives the building façade a tinkling, raindrop brilliance and suggests a cool retreat. This feeling of retreat is repeated in the interior conference room seen in Plate II, where the brise-soleil filters the light through the floor-to-ceiling window wall. A problem in large office buildings with all glass façades is the need to control the type of curtains and blinds which might be used in individual offices. Failure to consider this part of the design whole can ruin the façade. (*Curtis and Davis, Architects*)

*Plate I*

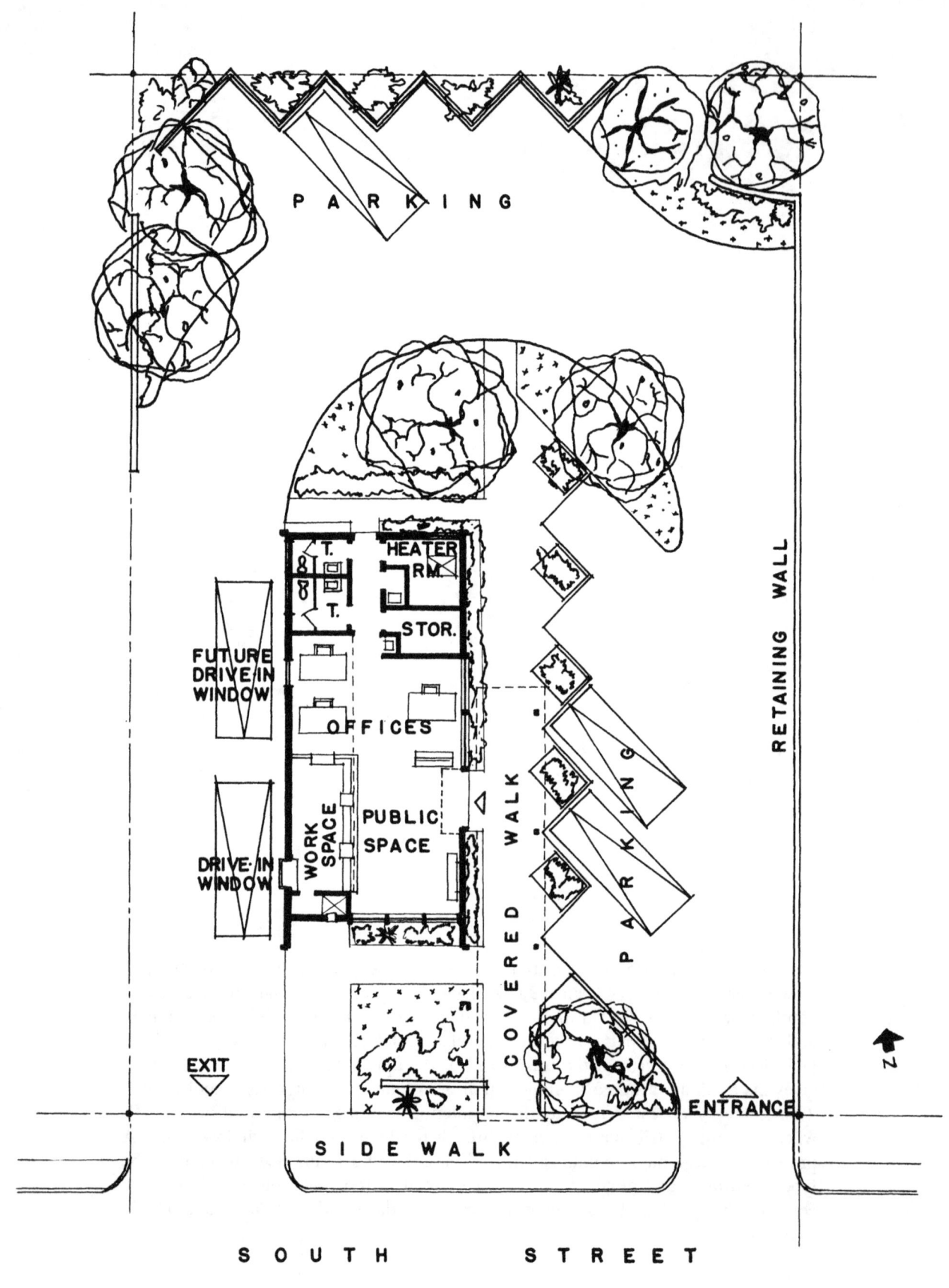

FLOOR & SITE PLAN
0  5  10  15  20  25 FEET

Plate II

Plate I

The site layout of this branch drive-in bank in Raleigh, North Carolina, is well organized. It allows cars to enter and park and when parking is exhausted to circle the building to the drive-in windows and then exit. At the same time there is space for other cars to pass and exit also. The first parking strip on the left of Plate III gives a diagonal parking area with easy access to a covered walk leading to the entrance of the bank. The pedestrian, who has not been forgotten, may enter from the street without crossing automobile lanes. This bank is additionally important because some attention has been paid to planting and landscaping. When the

115

Plate III

planting is mature it will become a pleasant relief from too much asphalt. It can be hoped that this bank with its well-modulated design may start a trend. (*F. Carter Williams, Architect*)

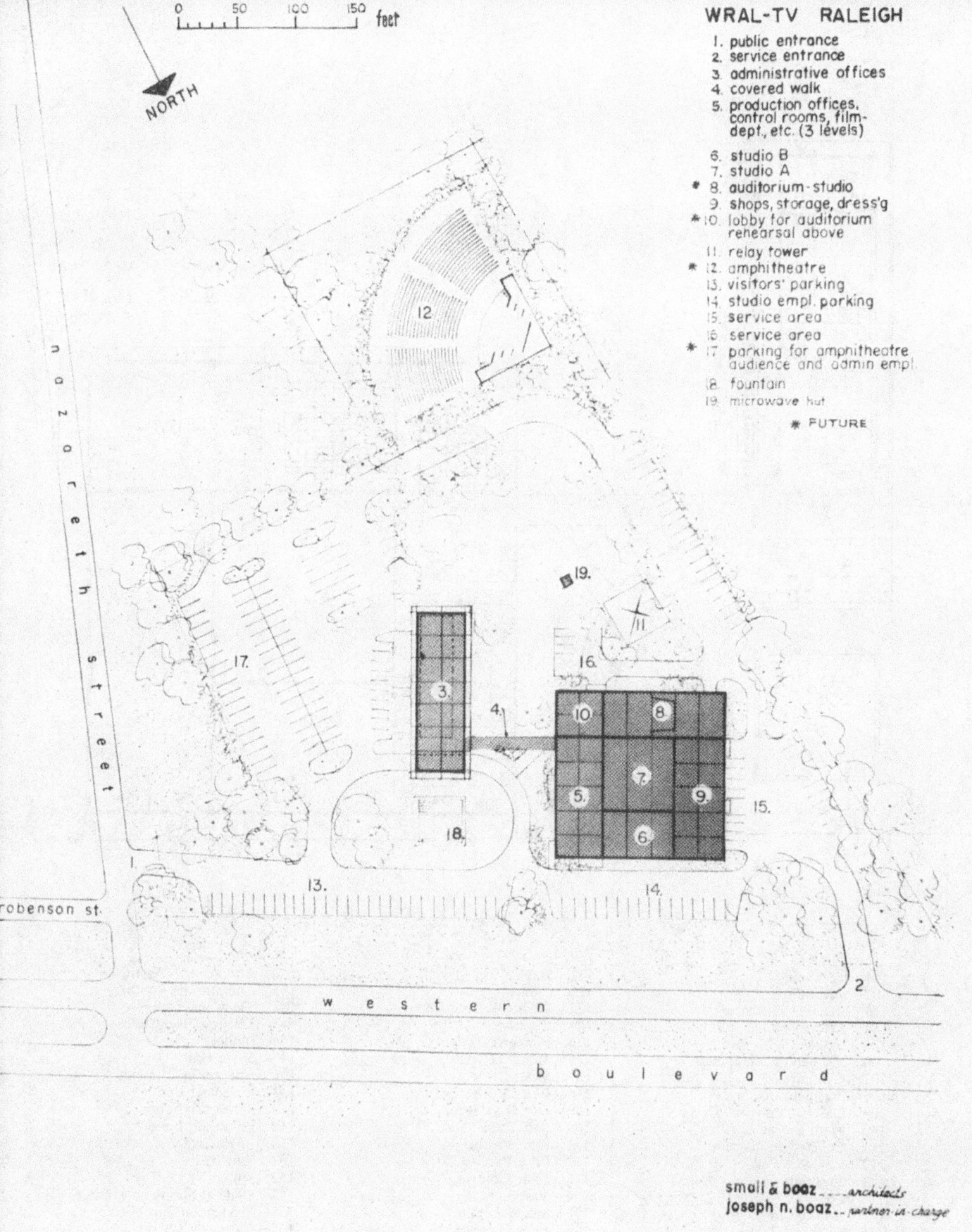

*Plate I*

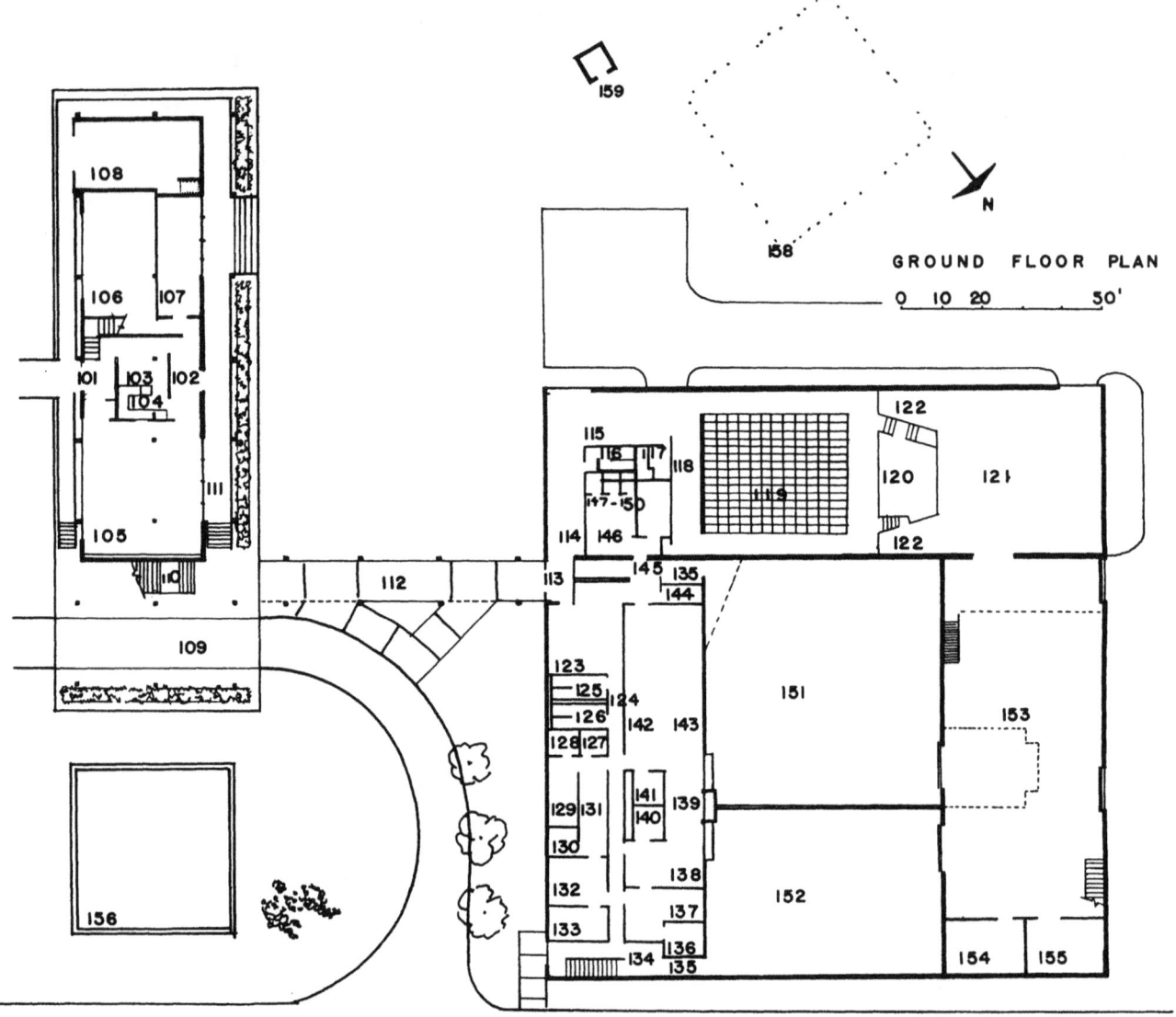

Plate II

| | | | | | |
|---|---|---|---|---|---|
| 101 | Vestibule | 121 | Stage | 140 | Announcer's Booth |
| 102 | Vestibule | 122 | Camera | 141 | Announcer's Booth |
| 103 | Vending Machines | 123 | Studio Waiting Room | 142 | TV Maintenance |
| 104 | Kitchen | 124 | Corridor | 143 | TV Equipment Racks |
| 105 | Lounge | 125 | Women's Toilet | 144 | Janitor |
| 106 | Mechanical Equipment | 126 | Men's Toilet | 145 | Spare Hall |
| 107 | Printing | 127 | Mixing Room | 146 | Announcer's Lounge |
| 108 | President's Garage | 128 | Wet Dark Room | 147 | Rehearsal Booth |
| 109 | Covered Entrance Drive | 129 | Dry Dark Room | 148 | Rehearsal Booth |
| 110 | Main Entrance Stair | 130 | Raw Film Stock | 149 | Rehearsal Booth |
| 111 | Covered Promenade | 131 | Film Processing | 150 | Engineering Supervisor |
| 112 | Covered Walk | 132 | Film Preview | 151 | Studio A |
| 113 | Vestibule | 133 | Film Storage | 152 | Studio B |
| 114 | Foyer | 134 | Vestibule | 153 | General Shop and Storage |
| 115 | Auditorium Lobby | 135 | Sound Lock | 154 | Production Supervisor |
| 116 | Women's Toilet | 136 | Film Director | 155 | Carpenter's Shop |
| 117 | Men's Toilet | 137 | Film Editing | 156 | Fountain |
| 118 | Sound Lock | 138 | Film Center | 158 | Relay Tower |
| 119 | Auditorium Seating | 139 | Master Control | 159 | Microwave Hut |
| 120 | Orchestra | | | | |

*Plate III*

The WRAL-TV buildings were completed in the spring of 1959 on a sloping site on the outskirts of Raleigh, North Carolina. The building group consists of two main elements (Plate I). The large element is the production building. It is connected by an open, two-level breezeway to the smaller administration building. The production structure houses two large studios (numbered 151 and 152 in Plate II). A large shop adjoins the studios and permits stage equipment to be shipped in from outside. On the other side of the studios are located the production offices, which include the main control center, dark rooms, film editing, and projection rooms. The production offices of this building are housed on two levels so that the main technical and control offices have visual access to the two high-ceilinged studios. Below the production offices is a third level housing the me-

Plate IV

chanical equipment. The structural system in this element of the building group consists of masonry bearing walls, steel beams, and openweb bar joists. Soundproofing in the studios is achieved by the application of a fiberglass blanket to the masonry walls, held in place by redwood battens. Year-round air-conditioning is achieved through accordion registers (Plate IV). The administration building is reinforced by concrete columns and flat slabs which project all around the building to give sun and weather protection to the walls. An entrance drive passes under this building, allowing pedestrians to alight under cover and ascend the stairs to the upper-level lobby. The upper floor plan of these buildings is not included here. (*Small and Boaz, Architects, Joseph N. Boaz, partner in charge*)

The architects of this New Orleans office building were aware of the interest the projected shadow of a tree will add to a building and were aware of the sunshade problems of the sunny South. In this building, the offices of the America-Fore Insurance Group, the low slanting sun encountered on east and west façades is shaded by the use of vertical fins as well as horizontal overhangs. In the early morning and the late afternoon these vertical fins throw slanting shadows across the façade to screen the windows. This treatment also gives a three-dimensional depth to the building and adds to its architectural interest. Name plates and signs are often difficult to integrate into the abstract formalism of contemporary architecture. This problem has been handled here with good taste. (*Curtis and Davis, Architects*)

No survey of Southern architecture would be complete without a contemporary cotton gin. The building here was designed and built in 1945 for the Georgia Institute of Genetics at Cartersville, Georgia. (*Aeck Associates, Architects*)

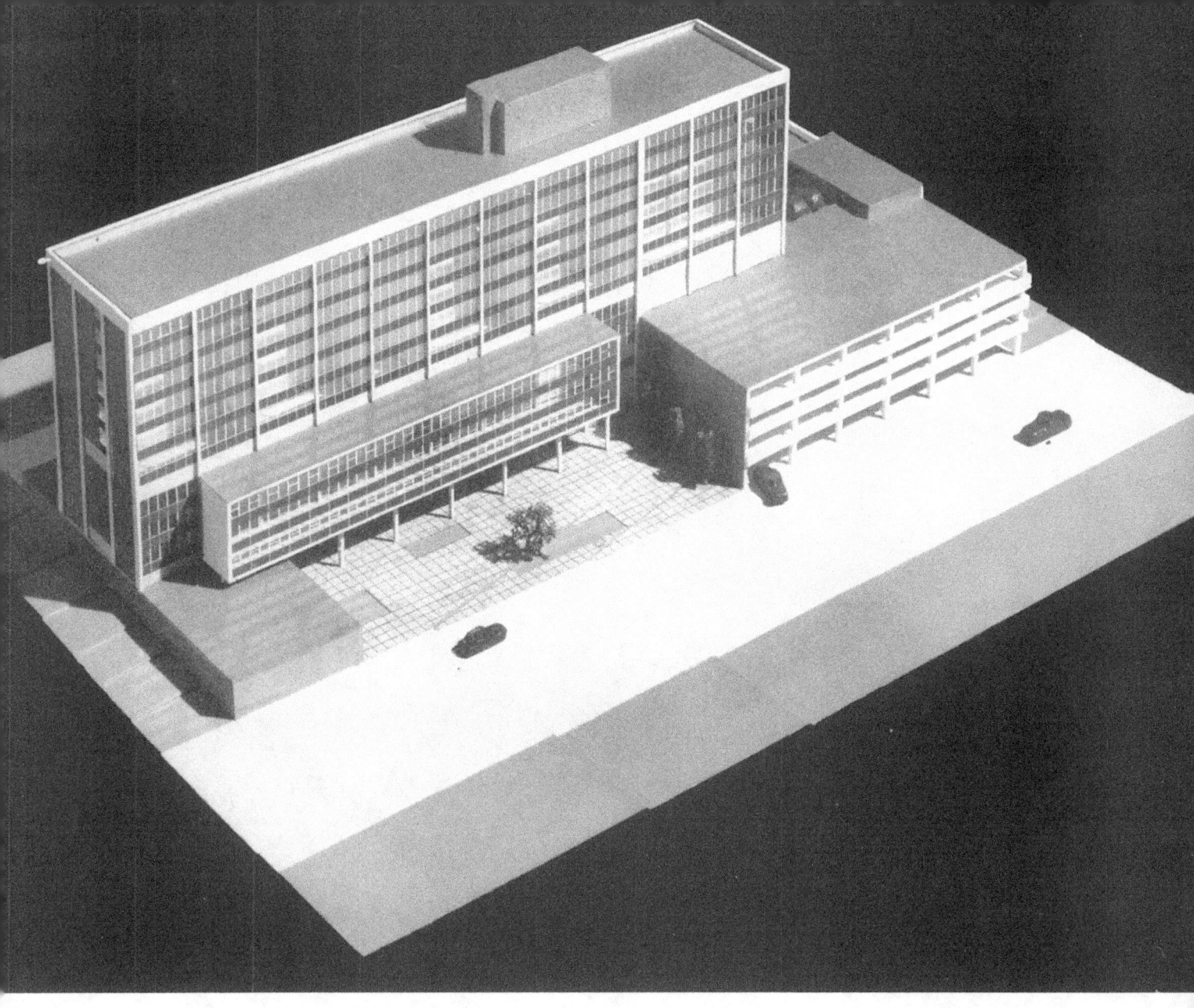

The South, in adopting contemporary architecture, continues the broad scope of its use. The office and apartment building shown here in model form is being erected in Memphis, Tennessee. The building expresses its steel-frame structural form in its treatment and rigidly uses assembly-line components for its window wall façades. (*A. L. Aydelott and Associates, Architects*)

Factory chimneys and fume exhausts have plagued city skylines since the industrial revolution. In this nuclear reactor exhaust stack for North Carolina State College in Raleigh, the architect has demonstrated that the required verticality of this type of functional unit can be treated as a piece of architectural sculpture and can even help enhance the over-all design. (*G. Milton Small, Architect*)

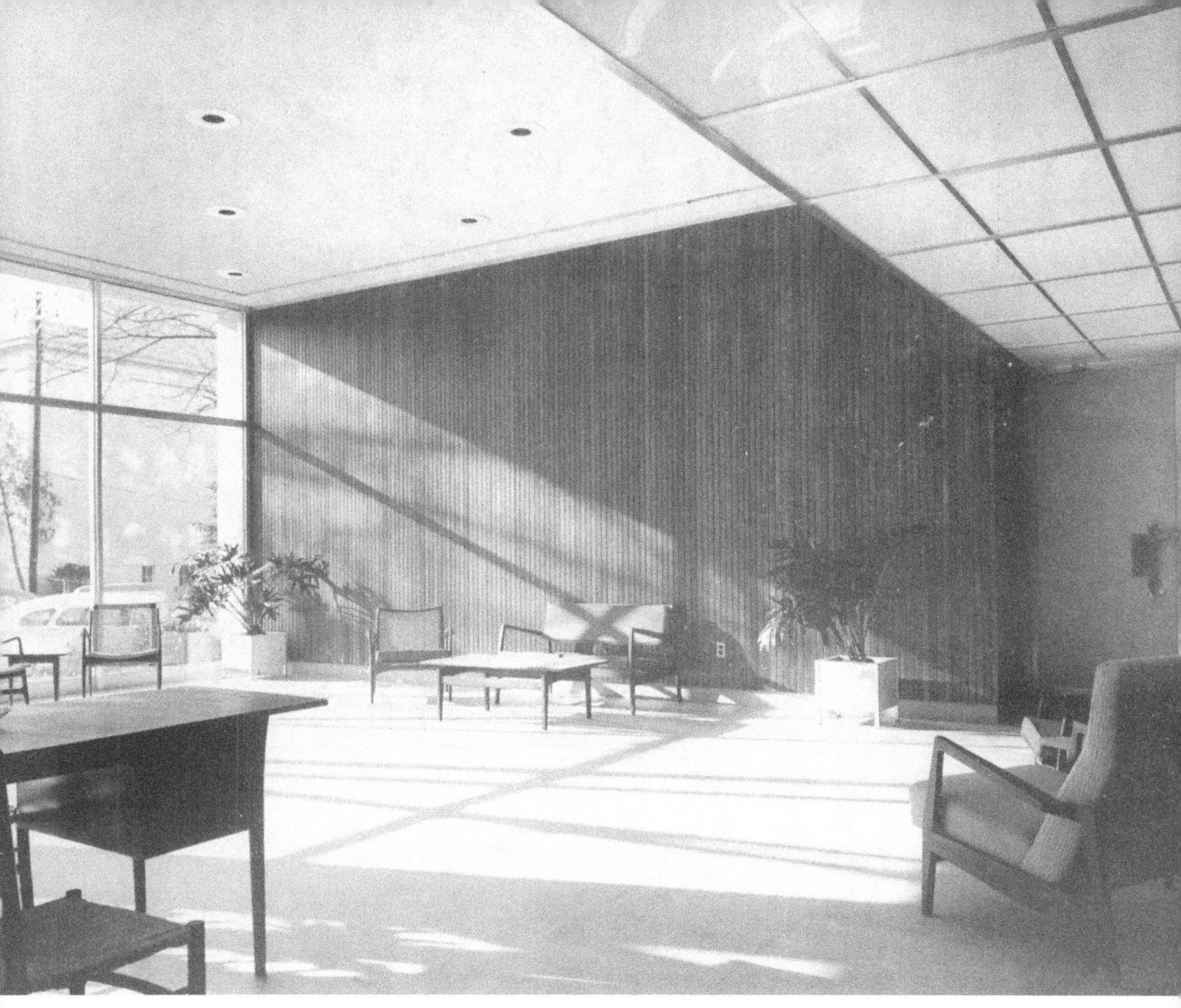

This lobby interior of the Associated Building in Columbia, South Carolina, demonstrates clean design approach to treating walls, ceilings, and floors as planes which modulate space simply and directly. The natural wood of the far wall contrasts with the white ceiling and the transparency of the window wall. The height is reduced by the dropped ceiling at the back of the lobby in order to bring it into scale with the normal door heights used in entering the office rooms. (*Lyles, Bissett, Carlisle, and Wolff, Architects*)

*Plate I*

The Sustan garment factory in New Orleans has been designed with careful attention to the production-line techniques of the modern factory. It should be noted that the long, continuous work tables in Plate II are well lighted by continuous, twin-tube florescent, industrial troffers. Also, the power outlet is a continuous trolley duct which enables a power unit to be plugged in anywhere along the production line so that the workers may move back and forth without having to trail electrical cords. This is a typical factory construction system in which light steel columns support rolled steel beams in one direction, and the latter in turn support prefabricated, long-span, open-web bar joists in the other direction. The roof deck is supported on this system. It may also be seen that the factory is air-conditioned by long spinal ducts placed longitudinally for convenient air distribution. The building from the exterior expresses the column spacing of the main structural system in the curtained masonry walls. The architects have added interest to the building by using a vaulted, shell-type entrance canopy and a free-form pierced wall. (*Curtis and Davis, Architects*)

*Plate II*

South Carolina and Virginia have been slower than the other Southern states in adapting to twentieth-century architecture. However, in the fall of 1958 construction started on this central office building and branch bank for the South Carolina National Bank in Columbia, South Carolina. The fact that a leading bank in the capital city retained the architectural services of a group of contemporary architects proves that contemporary architecture in the Deep South is here to stay. The building has a simple design scheme which is made up of the four-story office block on the right connected by a low entrance hall to the rectangular banking hall on the left. The importance of the banking hall is played up by the use of height and the simple glass fenestration, contrasting dramatically with the white-marble-veneered end wall of the office building. The entire building is trimmed on its exposed surfaces with this marble, while the window wall mullions are of aluminum and the glass itself is what is known as solar gray plate. This solar gray plate has a smoky, transparent appearance and it filters out much of the intensity of the sun with little sacrifice of its own transparency. (*Lyles, Bissett, Carlisle, and Wolff, Architects*)

*Plate I*

For the Eastgate Shopping Center in Chattanooga, Tennessee, the architects have approached the design problem with an understanding of the total environment. Here is one of the few shopping centers in the Southeast which not only pays some attention to the neighboring buildings and landscape features but also takes into account the use of trees (Plate II). An important feature of the plan is that supplies and deliveries can be routed in and out through the two underground ramps. Also, there is provision for pick-up by automobile customers. The various stores are grouped around a central mall dignified by a large, vertical tower. (*Toombs, Amisano, and Wells, Architects*)

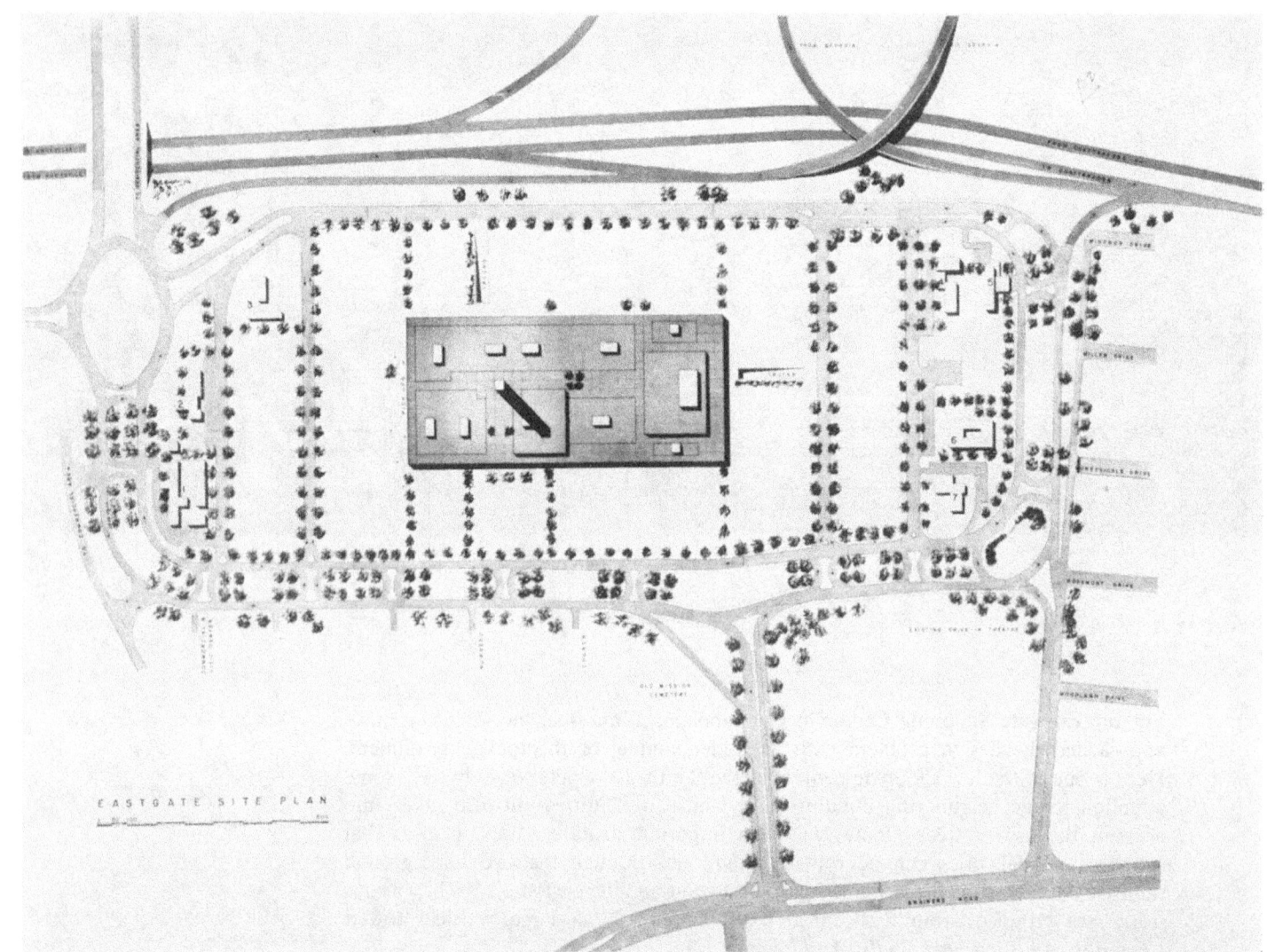

*Plate II*

*Plate III*

*Plate I*

Aeck Associates of Atlanta, Georgia, are pioneers in this type of concrete structure. In this parking deck, built in Atlanta, they have taken advantage of a sloping site to use an interlocking, split-level arrangement. In Plate I it may be seen that approximately half of the building has its four upper layers dovetailed at an intermediate level into the opposite part of the building. Such a device yields a considerable space-saving, as the hood of one automobile can be tucked between the trunk tail of its neighbors above and below it. The city, in its struggle to survive in the face of the parking problem, will be drawing more and more on the ingenuity of architects to design multi-deck parking units. (*Aeck Associates, Architects*)

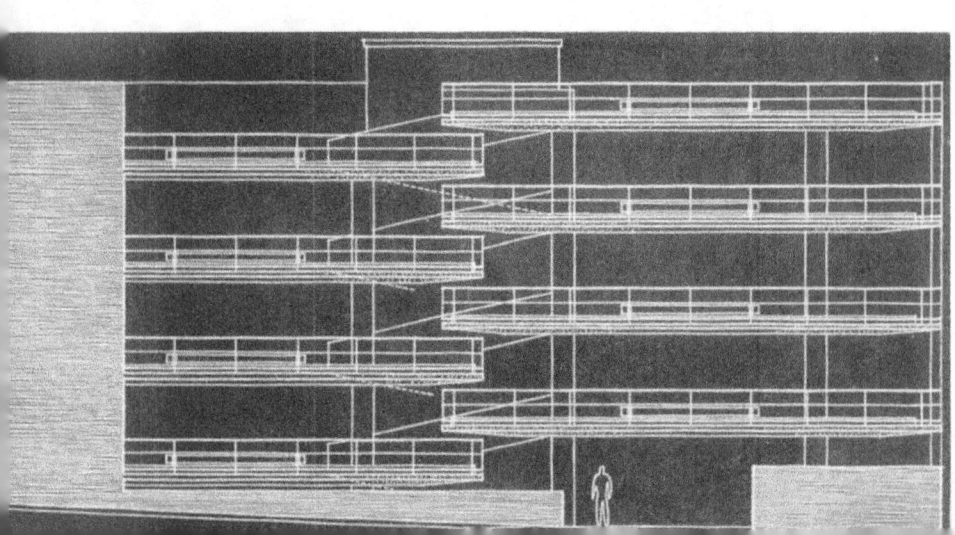

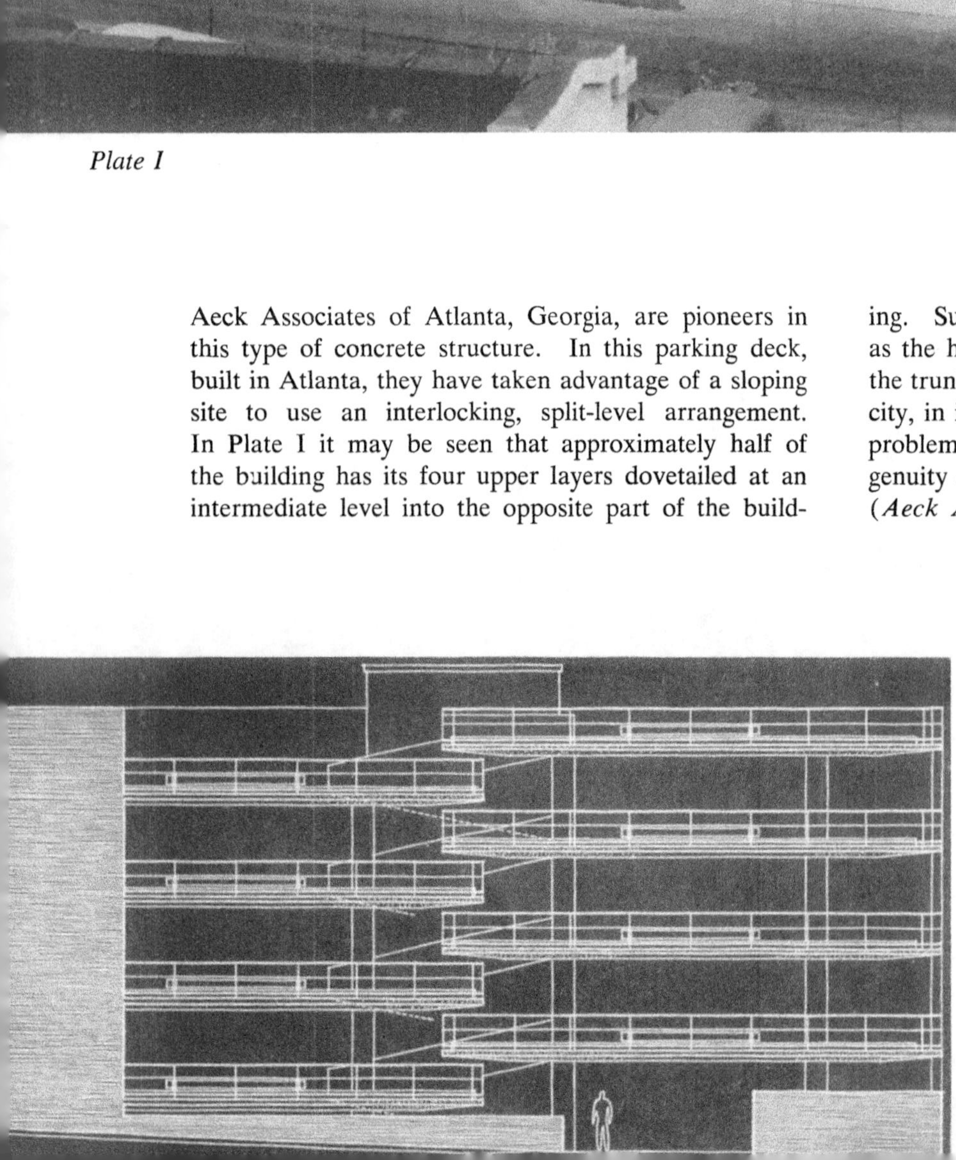

*Plate II*

Motel de Ville in New Orleans is a motel which has moved into the city and become a multi-story building, with cars relegated to the ground floor while the pedestrian accommodations and circulation takes place on the upper levels. The photographic view looks across from the lounge bar deck to the main part of the motel with the parked automobiles below. (*Charles R. Colbert, Architect*)

Plate I

The practice adopted by the large oil companies of standardizing gas station designs throughout the country might be architecturally acceptable if any of the standard designs had any merit. The developer of Forest Hills in Garner, North Carolina, decided that his residential neighborhood needed a good shopping center placed on a major highway which ran through his property. Here are two of the first buildings to go up on the site. The developer felt that a good gas station (Plate I) was a proper portal to a center designed to cater both to highway and neighborhood trade. This filling station was made to give a feeling of penetration through the building to the shopping center beyond. The accessory display area was sheathed in glass; it adjoins a covered space where motorists can sit and enjoy refreshments from vending machines. The toilets are also under covered approaches, not at the back like outhouses. The building has wide overhangs and has been made impressive in length by the addition of the developer's office at one end. Because of this large overhang, any number of motorists may be sheltered. The building is eye-catching because of its simplicity, in contrast to the usual filling station gaudiness. It may be approached by cars from all directions. The food store (Plate II) had to be built to stand alone for a while until other buildings could be added. Therefore, viewed from any direction, it is a good building. The structural system of rolled-steel members, exposed and painted to integrate into the design, continue on the same module from the main section of the building out over the covered walkway. The sales area is a large, flexible space bordered on the back by storage, and food preparation facilities, utilities (the building is heated and cooled by air-to-air pumps), and loading accommodations. The subtle suspension of the entrance canopy lends both dramatic impact and better shelter for shoppers. Although the site was a former cotton field without trees, the architects planned for future parking shade around this building. And when other building elements are added, "pedestrian only" shops with full shade and screen planting are to be integrated into the center. (*Waugh and Sawyer, Architects*)

*Plate II*

Heavy earth-moving equipment has become an important part of the everyday economy of the Southeast. This equipment company building in Raleigh, North Carolina, houses the head offices, the sales room, and machine shop for a state-wide distribution and servicing company. Even bulldozers can assume a glamorous appearance when properly placed in a good building. (*George Matsumoto and G. Milton Small, Architects*)

Plate I

Architect Victor Lundy of Sarasota, Florida, is as much at home with concrete shell structures as he is with laminated wood. His architectural scope is well expressed in the bird's-eye view (Plate I) of the Warm Mineral Springs Inn at Sarasota. Lundy boldly uses about seventy-five identical, hyperbolic, parabolic concrete plates measuring fourteen feet and five inches square, placed on seventy-five vertical concrete columns

Plate II

of alternating height. The result is a space checkerboard when seen from above; when seen from below, the extra interest of the columns, the penetration of light, and the play of silhouette confirm the opinion that architect Lundy is indeed a space-time architect. The use of shells in this design shows extreme sophistication in concept, yet the building was constructed by unskilled labor. Plate IV shows a part plan and a vertical section through part of the structure. In the part plan the shaded part represents the concrete plates which are placed at the lower level and the unshaded, the upper level. In Plate III the interior view shows the intriguing effect which natural daylight gives to the ceiling. (*Victor Lundy, Architect*)

*Plate III*

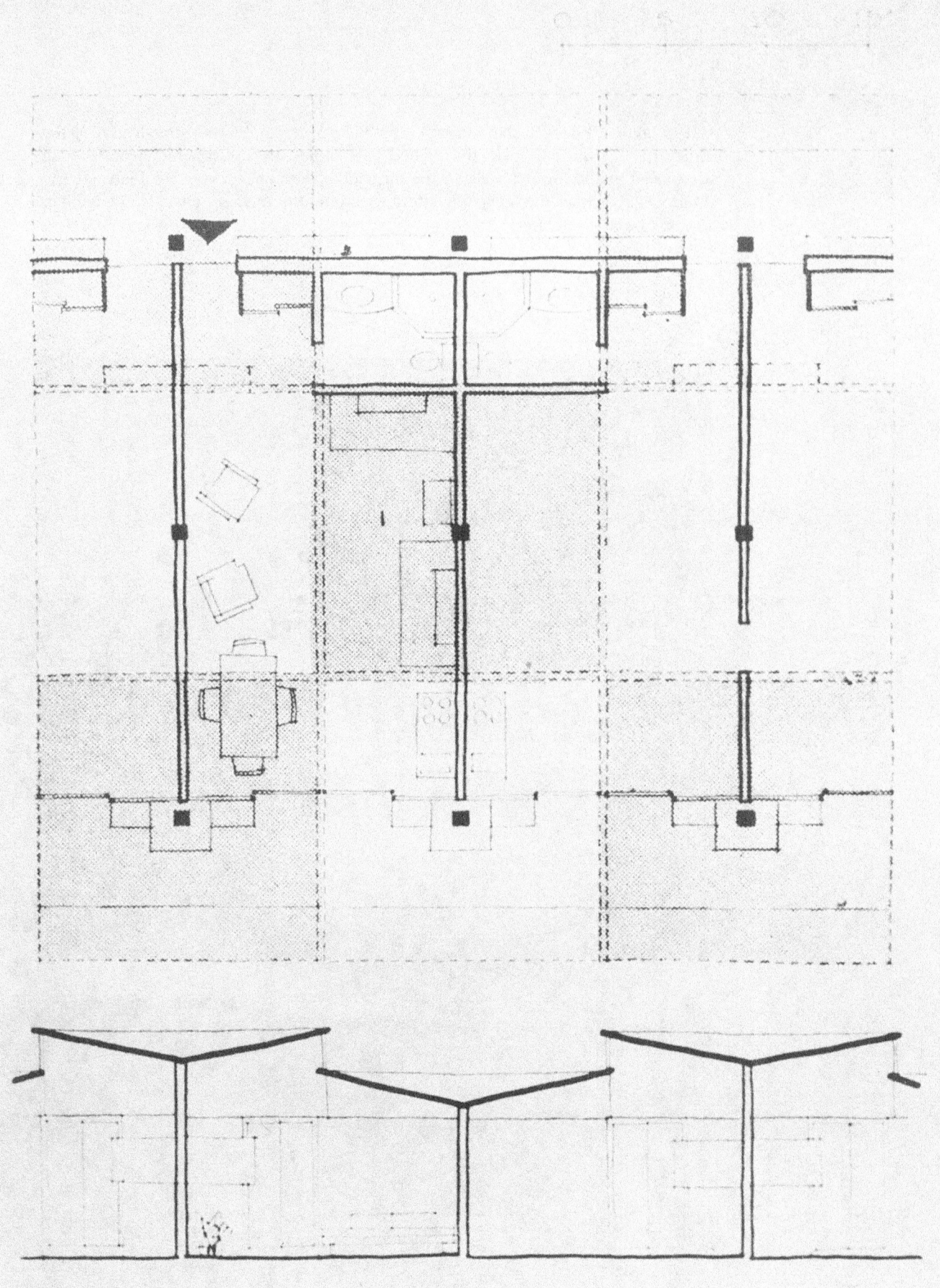

*Plate IV*

# VI. Trends and Purposes

THE extremes of directions which architecture is now taking may be likened to the points of an equilateral triangle. On one of these extremities is modern Palladianism (a term which we have associated with the work of Mies van der Rohe), so beautifully expressed in the Reynolds Aluminum Building at Richmond, Virginia. Another is exemplified in the Bee Ridge Presbyterian Church in Sarasota, Florida, which shows the range available to the architect who uses his materials in a "romantic" way. At the third point of the triangle is a building designed to meet the problem of exploding college enrollment, shortage of land, and scarcity of professors. This classroom building for North Carolina State College, soon to be built, was developed as part of a master plan for the total future architectural environment of that institution. Each of the three architectural trends is important, and perhaps all have or will have validity as specific architectural solutions in our present society. It is the buildings which fall in between these that create the potential danger of a poor architectural milieu.

For example, there is the modern Palladian façade which uses the prefabricated window wall as a sterile design formula. It is often a poor imitation of the United Nations Building or Lever House, and variants of it are beginning to appear in too many new school buildings in the Southern region. This kind of architecture is casting a shadow on the beauty and validity of good designs which employ this medium in a proper functional way and with proper sensitivity. In fact, if this misuse continues over the next ten years it promises to run the Mies van der Rohe school of architecture into the ground, just as the pseudo-Georgian Revival of the 1920's and 1930's destroyed any further usefulness in neo-classical architecture. It is a good sign, however, that this indiscriminate window-wall architecture is now losing ground in the architectural schools.

Another architectural development which could become a cliché is the shell. The structural analysis of the shell form demands advanced engineering competence. Contributions to its development have been made by a number of engineers, including Pier Luigi Nervi of Italy, Félix Candela of Mexico, Felix James Samuely of London, and Paul Weidlinger of New York. While these men tend to favor the use of concrete and concrete shells, Buckminster Fuller, the American engineer, is having a profound influence upon design with light-metal space frames used as dome structures. Although his ideas have not yet made their full impact on the practicing architect, they are being felt among the more recent student graduates.

The architecture of the future may develop into a battle between the molded-concrete shell structures of Nervi and the space frames of Fuller and his followers. Structurally both are significant because both can be designed as self-sufficient units. The dome structure does not necessarily rely upon outside force for its structural integrity, and sometimes this is true of the concrete shell. Both could exist as structures without relying for stability on the pull of gravity. Both systems are products of twentieth-century investigation.

A shell used as a natural consequence of the right structural solution can be magnificent. Architect Aeck's Pavilion Restaurant at Dinemountain, Georgia, and architect Lundy's Inn at Sarasota, Florida, are examples of important shell structures. Their importance comes from their use of repetitive units, which permit a construction technique of the greatest utility in a highly industrialized society. Other significant structural forms are the hyperbolic parabolic roof of the Catalano house, which has a warped surface as a stressed skin, and the catenary cable roof of the North Carolina State Fair pavilion, which uses two concrete arches to oppose the tension of the cables. Both of these buildings are in Raleigh, North Carolina. Fuller's geodesic dome, which has been developed sometimes as a lattice structure and sometimes as a repetitive series of prefabricated modular shells, is represented by a fine Southern example in the Unitank structure at Baton Rouge, Louisiana.

And just as modern physics and its application by engineers have brought challenging structural and sculptural forms into the vocabulary of the contemporary architect, so they have also produced a dazzling variety of new technical improvements in the application of thermodynamics, hydraulics, acoustics, and electronics to the problems of controlling the human environment. The architect of today can approach his classic role as a creator of spatial forms only after he has mastered a variety of new techniques for lighting, heating, air-conditioning, water supply, and sewage disposal. The very variety of the new techniques and concepts available can lead to a kind of sterility; and it is small wonder that the contemporary architect occasionally feels bogged down in scientific innovation and machine production.

But there can be no doubt as to the necessity facing the Southern architect today to master the new design concepts and the new techniques. He is living in an age of explosive population increase and in a region in which there is the additional factor of a vast shift from the country to the town and city. It is no longer sufficient for the architect to be the interpreter of the environment and culture of his time in the individual buildings he creates. The architect can meet the challenges of the day only by becoming responsible for the design of the total physical environment in our future town and country development. This calls for regional planning, the planning of subregions, cities, towns, and communities. The architect cannot act alone at the regional planning level, but he can become an important member of a regional planning team which would have to include many other professionals, such as sociologists, conservationists, land planners, agriculturists, and civil, mechanical, and chemical engineers, to say nothing of professionals concerned with education, health, and welfare. The architect-planner would first have to grasp the problem at the regional level, as the basis for the work of the town planner-architect at the city or town-country level. The design of individual but integrated buildings could then be handled by practicing architects at the local level.

In order to achieve this kind of thinking, the architectural schools of the South will have to undergo a revolution, or at least a change of emphasis in the training of some of their students. The present tendency is to orient all students toward a personal approach to architectural problems. Too much emphasis is given to the idea that each student might be a budding architectural virtuoso rather than a professional socio-architect concerned with the inter-related problems of man's total environment.

The South is fortunate in having within its own area, in the Tennessee Valley Authority, one of the world's outstanding examples of regional planning. This project, sponsored by the federal government under the New Deal, has come in for much political criticism, and its importance has sometimes been clouded by political bickering. It is unimportant now whether the project was financed by private or government enterprise—the important fact is that it was done at all and on such a masterful and magnificent scale. If viewed objectively, it ranks as one of the modern wonders of the world and has become a model to be copied not only by ourselves but by our friends and enemies around the world. TVA is a magnificent illustration of total environmental planning and successful operation under such planning. It is a pity that the architectural profession in the new South has not organized itself so as to be able to work within the framework of such an enterprise.

Nevertheless, in the South today some outstanding planning is being done on a smaller scale. Already mentioned in this volume are the planning activities of universities and colleges in the South. Also, some good redevelopment of blighted city areas is going on in such cities as New Orleans and Tallahassee—to mention only two. These are only beginnings in meeting the critical needs of the South's expanding urbanism.

By way of summary it might be said that from the time of its first settlements at Jamestown, St. Augustine, and New Orleans, the South evinced a strong and independent architectural evolution, which maintained itself through the colonial and national periods to the end of the nineteenth century. The architectural vulgarity of the early twentieth century which has swamped the older regionalism is the joint product of the production line in industry, extraordinary technological progress, and a crass commercial spirit in our economic and social attitudes. For their efforts to think through to a new architecture that will make full use of the new techniques and concepts and that will relate them to our real human needs, we owe a debt to the pioneers of the architecture of contemporary cultures and to the new architects who have taken the torch from them.

Regionalism in architecture is no longer a creative and active force in the South. In fact, it cannot flourish in any highly industrialzed and economically developing country, for it sustains itself only in the environment of the handcraftsman. The new architecture in the South is here to stay, but it, too, suffers from the danger of becoming an architecture of clichés. The South has a long road to travel before it can recapture graciousness within its new architectural forms. It can never be recaptured except by a proper integration of scientific achievements within the needs of the individual. And that is possible only for a people mature enough to accept the necessity for rational planning of the whole human environment.

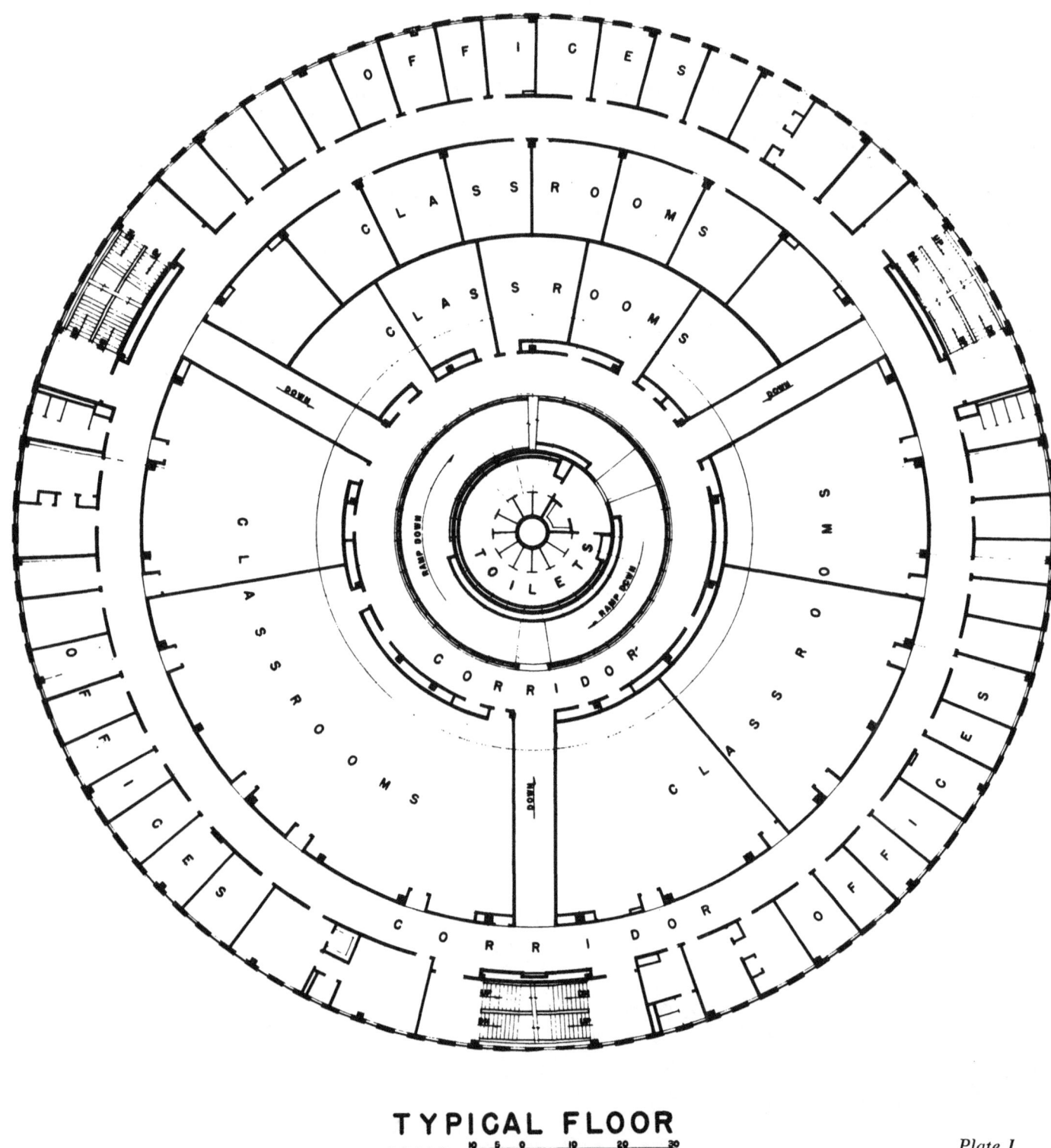

**TYPICAL FLOOR**

SCALE

*Plate 1*

The model and plans of this classroom building are shown in this book because they seem to represent the beginning of a new type of building design in the relation of the building to its total environment. In its final form the building will be part of a complex of a circular and a square building, the first housing large lecture

Plate II

courses and the second, small seminar classes. The idea behind these designs is to use the senior faculty to lecture to large groups of students in the circular building, while the junior faculty uses the small classrooms of the square building for group meetings of the same classes. Ultimately this building will serve as the general classroom building for the eight schools on the North Carolina State campus and will be mainly used for social studies and mathematics, which are required

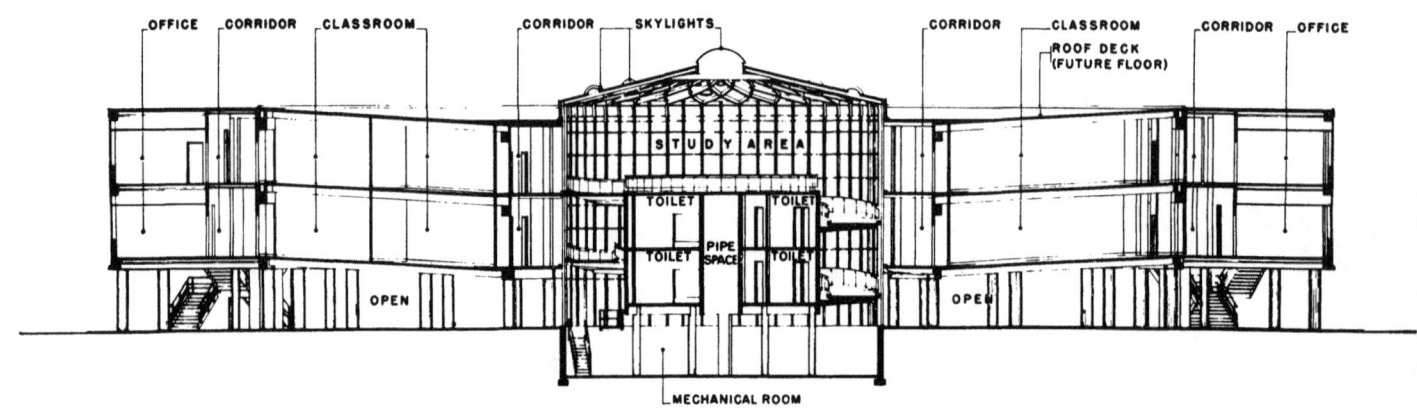

*Plate III*

courses for all students. At present campus enrollment is six thousand and is expected to reach fifteen thousand by 1975. The view of the model in Plate II shows the building in its first stage—a two-story building which is really three "soup-plate" shaped disks arranged one above the other. At three points around the periphery are exit stairs which drop to the open ground floor. Arranged around the horizontal rim of the soup-plate are the individual faculty offices and departmental offices. On the sloping part of the disk are located the lecture rooms, while the inner flat center has another circular corridor which connects to a spiral ramp floating around an inner vertical cylinder which forms the toilets for the building. The classrooms will be artificially lighted and year-round air-conditioned. (*Holloway, Reeves, and Waugh, Architects, Raymond Sawyer, Associated*)

The Union Tank Car Company commissioned this geodesic dome in Baton Rouge, Louisiana, as a roundhouse and maintenance structure for its cars. Its dome is, in a sense, a spherical truss; in order to function as a truss it must have an inner chord and outer chord system which, in this case, must of necessity follow the spherical form. The inner chord is a continuous steel shell made from 11-gauge sheet steel formed from a series of involuted hexagons. The outer chord is made up of a space-frame hexagon system which compliments the steel inner shell. It may be seen from the photograph that the inner shell seems to float within the lattice work of the outer structure. The inner plates of the shell act as the inner members of the truss. The beauty of this system is that it is, in effect, a cellular structure consisting of octahedrons which are formed by the inner hexagon cells on the inner surface and by the hexagon struts on the outer surface. For this reason the dome may be erected as a series of facets and does not need to have form work to support it. The seams joining the inner hexagons are welded as the frame is erected, and because of the geometry a hemispherical form results. Of architectural importance in this dome is the fact that it is made up of 320 identical hexagonal subassemblies; when put together the steel inner plates not only are structural but they also provide the ceiling and weatherproofing membrane. The dome was designed by Synergetics Incorporated, a firm founded by Buckminster Fuller. One of the driving forces behind this firm is a talented architect who for six years was on the School of Design faculty of North Carolina State College, James W. Fitzgibbon. Much of the geometry was developed by Duncan R. Stuart, at present a member of the School of Design faculty. (*Synergetics Incorporated, Architect*)

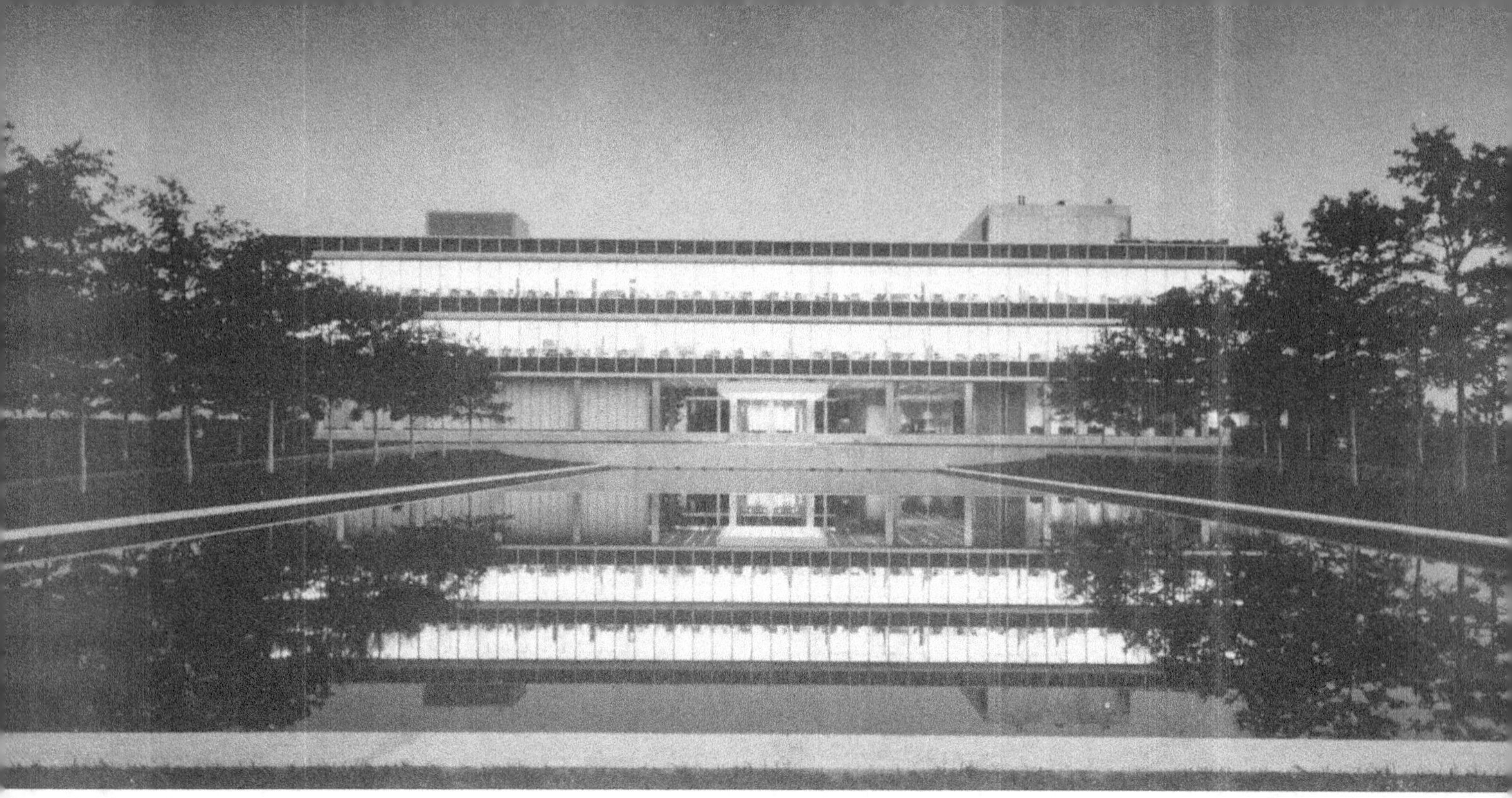

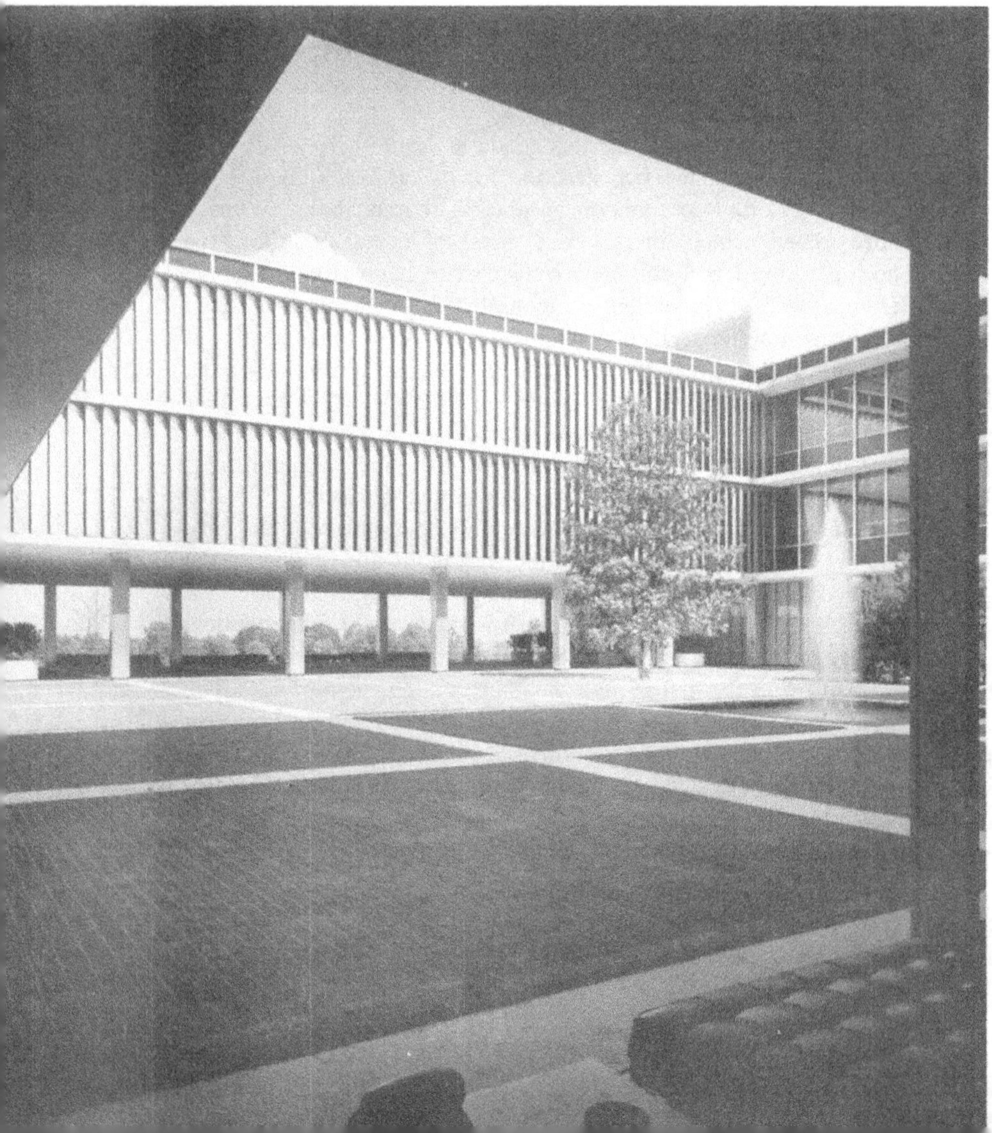

In 1958 the Reynolds Metals Company moved its main office from Louisville, Kentucky, to Richmond, Virginia. The elegant new 11½ million-dollar headquarters building continues the trend of the contemporary corporate client in constructing a prestige building by a creative architect of international talent, reputation, and distinction. The Virginia Museum of Fine Art in Richmond proudly dubbed the building "the finest since Thomas Jefferson." Then, in the fear of state-wide criticism by the architectural profession, it asked twelve national leaders in architecture to endorse its apparently rash contention. Of the twelve, all but Frank Lloyd Wright supported the Museum's notion, and the Museum boldly gave the architects a first-rate and magnificent exhibition of the office's more important work. The principal building elements are arranged in shapely classical manner, with a symmetrical approach down a formal mall. A lower story rises out of the solid stylobate, giving a temple-like appearance to the composition. In keeping with current Southern practice in large buildings, the structure is completely air-conditioned. Two nearly equal parking spaces flank the pool mall and give space for about 450 cars. The site, some seven miles from the Richmond business district because of lower land cost, permitted generous spacing on the grounds with the provision of some very handsome landscape architecture. The quiet classical serenity of the exterior with the modulated curtain wall and mobile outside aluminum sun-louvres on the east and west is carried into the interior with equal elegance. The colors, materials, furnishings, and accessories are in harmony with the classical concept and the precise detailing. Paintings selected with the help of the architects by Picasso, Le Corbusier, Steinberg, Albers, and others complete the total statement. (*Skidmore, Owings and Merrill, Architects, design partner, Gordon Bunshaft, associated with David Hughes*)

Plate II

This restaurant in a Georgian resort area fronts on a swimming lake. Plate I shows the free tented canopied effect which these inverted concrete cones give to the interior space which they delineate. The design has a playful free rhythm which gives it the *joie de vivre* that a place of this kind should have. The Japanese-type lanterns, the sky showing through circular forms between the concrete umbrellas, the flags in the breeze above the building all these contribute to the over-all lightness of spirit. A significant trend in architecture is apparent in the structural system of this building. Each one of the inverted cones is cast on one form and then lifted into place by a crane and balanced on its concrete column. Once three of these had been set up in a triangular position they were joined together by the triangular horizontal piece seen in the top right of Plate I. This gives structural stability to the system, and subsequent cones can be added in the same manner indefinitely. This trend of using stressed skin concrete shell construction was developed in Europe over the last twenty years and has only recently been introduced into the United States. While large stressed skin domes and shells which require poured-in-place concrete are not valid in our highly mechanized economy because of the high labor cost of constructing the once-used forms, the repetitive structural forms as seen in this building are a fine example of the proper use of concrete in a society as highly industrialized as the Southeast is becoming. (*Aeck Associates, Architects*)

Plate I

The Ezra Meir house in Raleigh, North Carolina, is unimportant as a house but brilliantly significant as a twentieth-century trend in architectural construction. The form is inspired by the impact of the constructivist sculptor on the early design training and thinking of young architects. The constructivist has become concerned with the generation of compound curves by the use of straight lines passed across or within regular geometric forms in a stroboscopic manner. Architect Catalano had a brilliant idea when he applied this linear development to make his triple-layered, warped-roof skin out of regular straight tongue-and-groove flooring. The roof form was generated by a simple warped parallelogram which had its two opposite points on the ground, and these were opposed by two heavy concrete buttresses which were connected underneath the floor by steel tension cables. The other two points were up in the air, and the whole was outlined with steel I-beams to which the end edges of the sandwich-type wood shell were connected. (*Eduardo Catalano, Architect*)

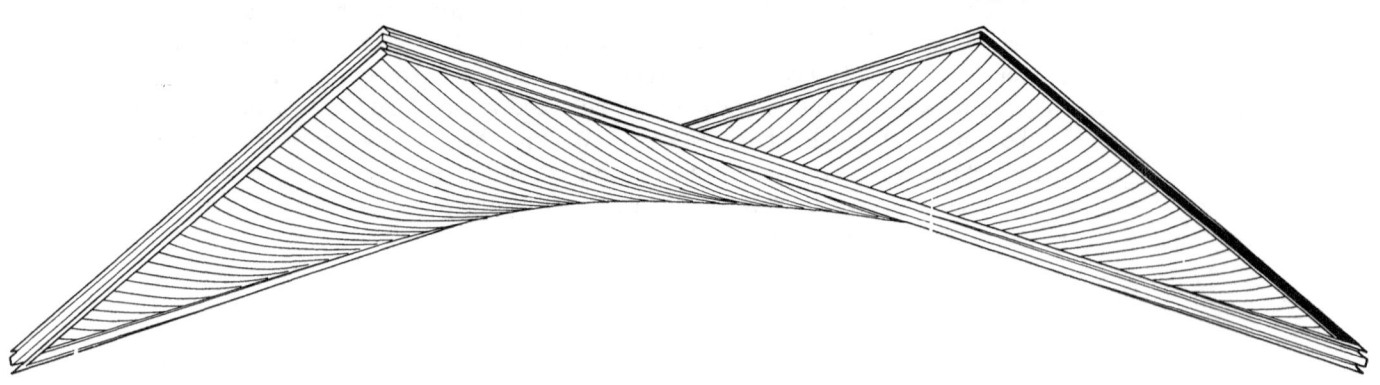

152

Plate I

The Bee Ridge Presbyterian Church in Sarasota, Florida, achieves a simple beauty by the brilliant handling of the main roof structure and the delicacy of the screen walls which enfold the church. At no place do these screen walls touch the roof. They are separated from it by transparent glass which is sufficiently protected by the generous overhangs to cut down any glare and thus to give the church a diffused interior light. The design of the screen walls themselves is ingenious: architect Lundy designed a special L-shaped block (Plate V) which is so cleverly bonded that it gives a changing brilliance to the walls as the sun moves around. The exterior walls have the feeling of an eighteenth-century chandelier or perhaps a Harry Bertoia sculpture when brightly lighted. This is well illustrated in Plate II. Here the amazing difference in texture of the two wall surfaces is most apparent when light strikes them at different angles at the same time. This could be called four-dimensional design, because it introduced light, space, and motion into the building so that the texture changes every moment. The basic materials in this church are three—wood, cement-concrete (floor, masonry, mortar), and glass. With these three age-old materials and with full knowledge of modern technology for laminated wood structure, the architect has created a building which sings out aesthetically and points toward a future trend in design even while it maintains symbolically a firm link with past ages. (*Victor Lundy, Architect*)

Plate III

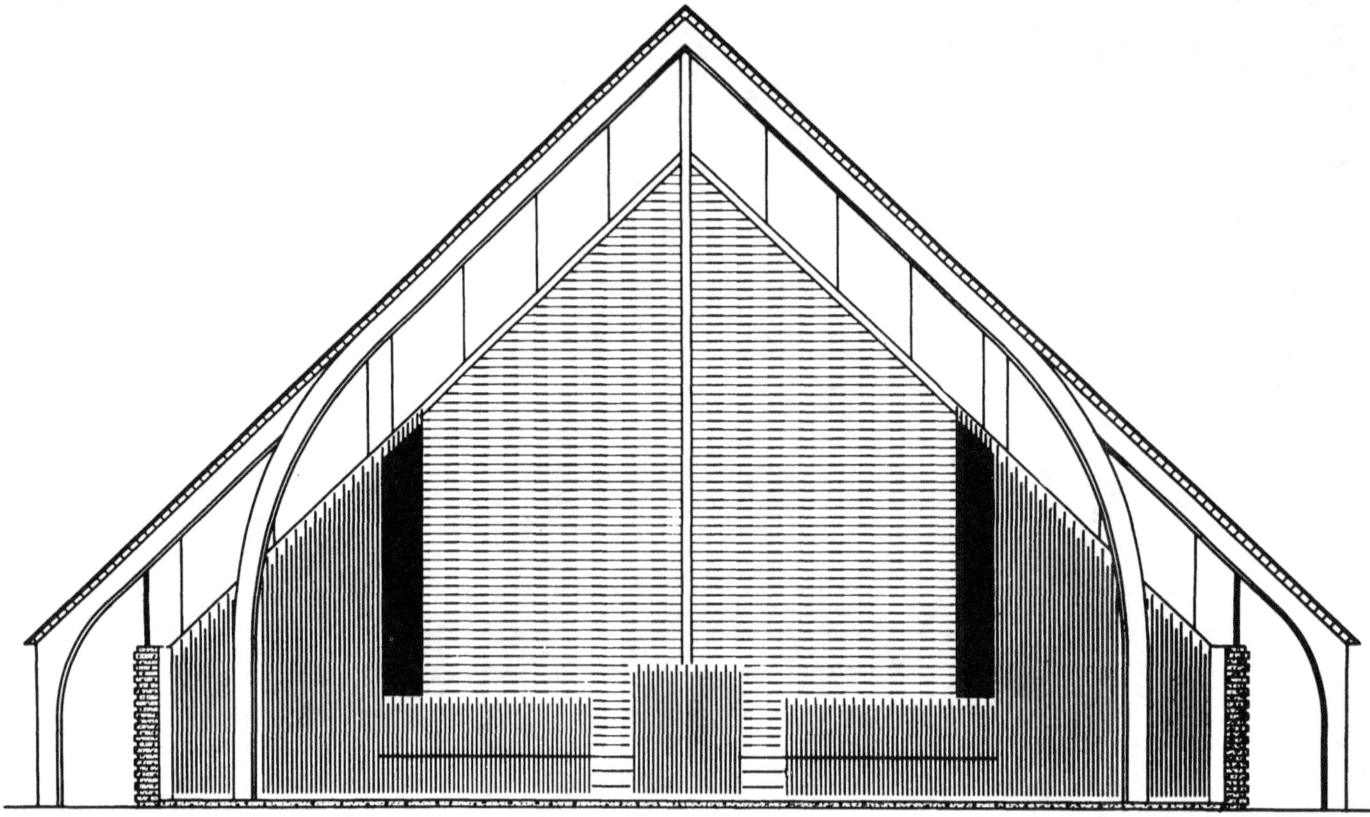

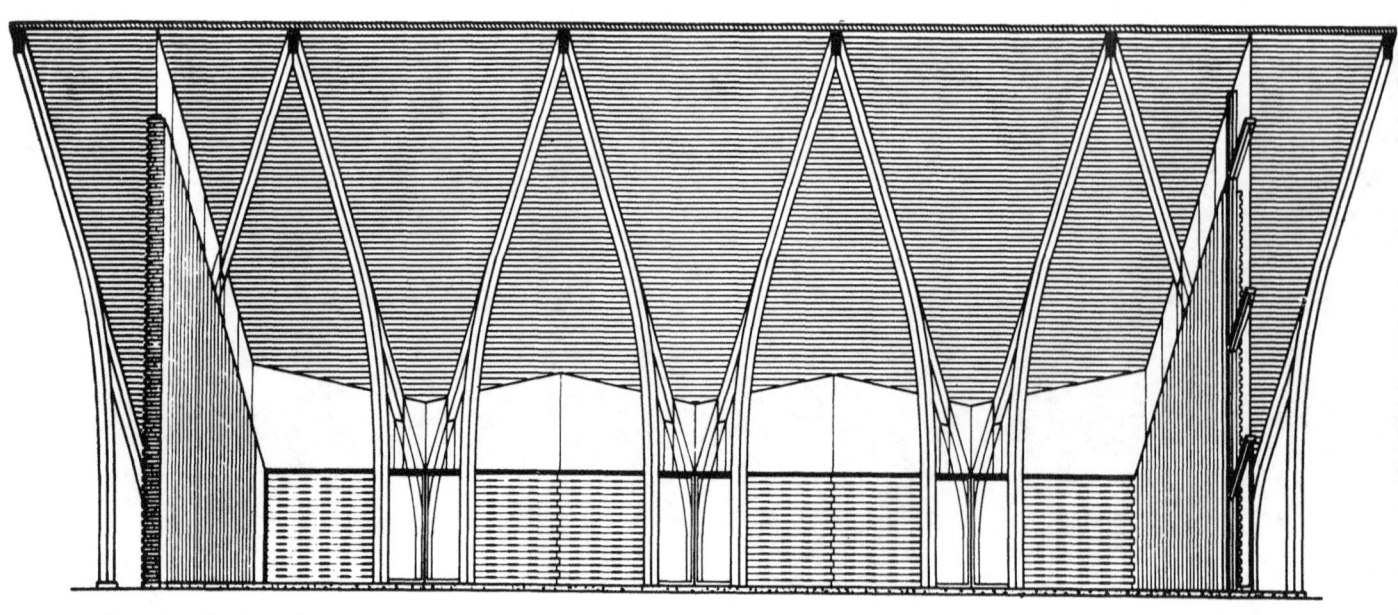

Transverse section

Longitudinal section

Plate IV

late V

MASONRY WALL ELEVATION
FULL SIZE
MASONRY UNIT
A-A
PLAN
0
1
2
3
4
5

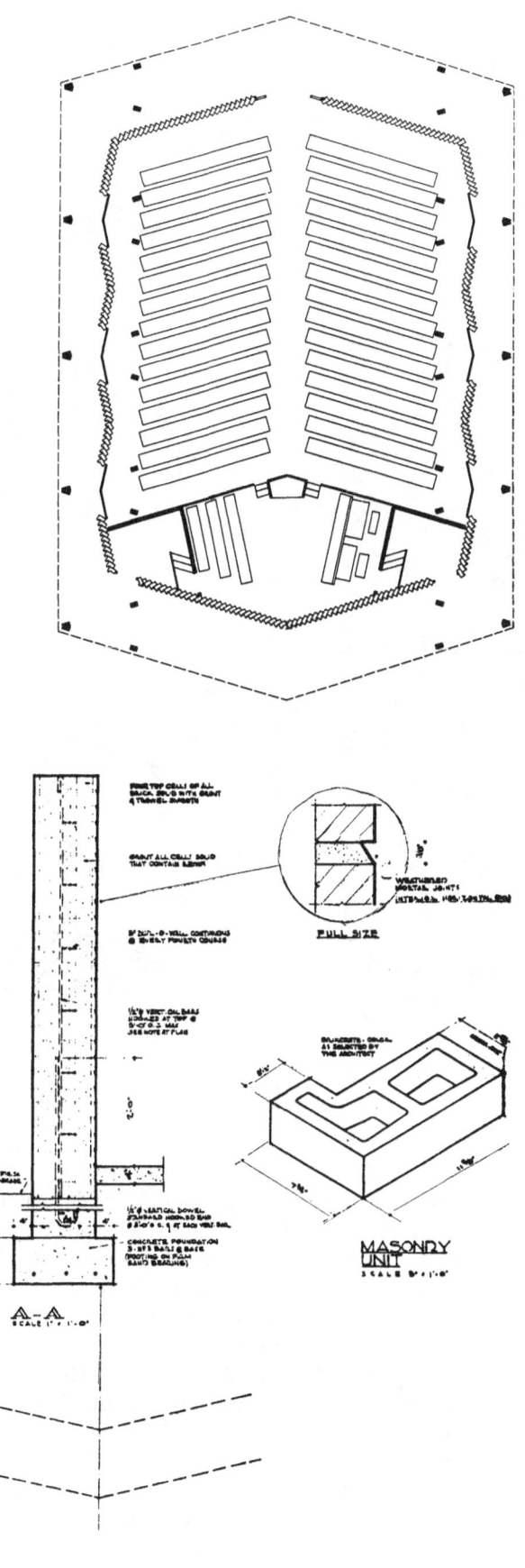

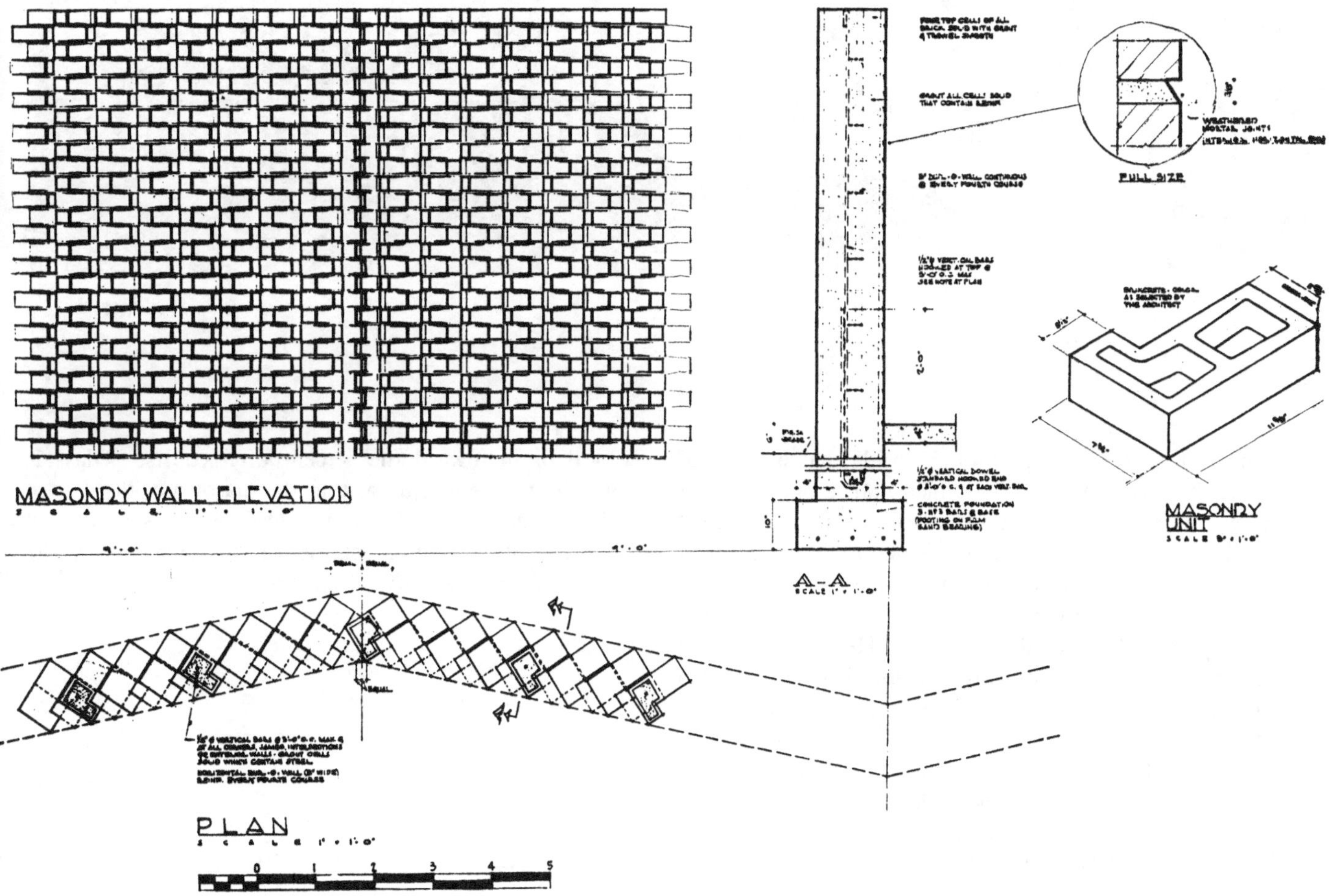

*Plate I*

The Herron house in Sarasota, Florida, has a sense of the light touch in its design which makes one feel that it would be a delightful place to live in. Architect Victor Lundy has taken six laminated arches and cantilevered wood arch frames and decked them over to make a roof canopy under which he organized the floor plan with a singular freedom. He astutely avoids having the powerful structural sculpturism of the form dominate the privacy of the various divisions of the house. The dining-living area, while circular in plan, penetrates through the entire house by the development of screened porches on either side of it. The bedrooms and the den are located at the four diagonal corners of the square and thus enjoy the openness of looking outward or in toward the screen-porch courts. Glass is used in the bedrooms so that the masonry walls do not violate the sculptural form. The design is successful because of the zoning of the various elements of the plan. (*Victor Lundy, Architect*)

*Plate*

Plate III

Plate IV

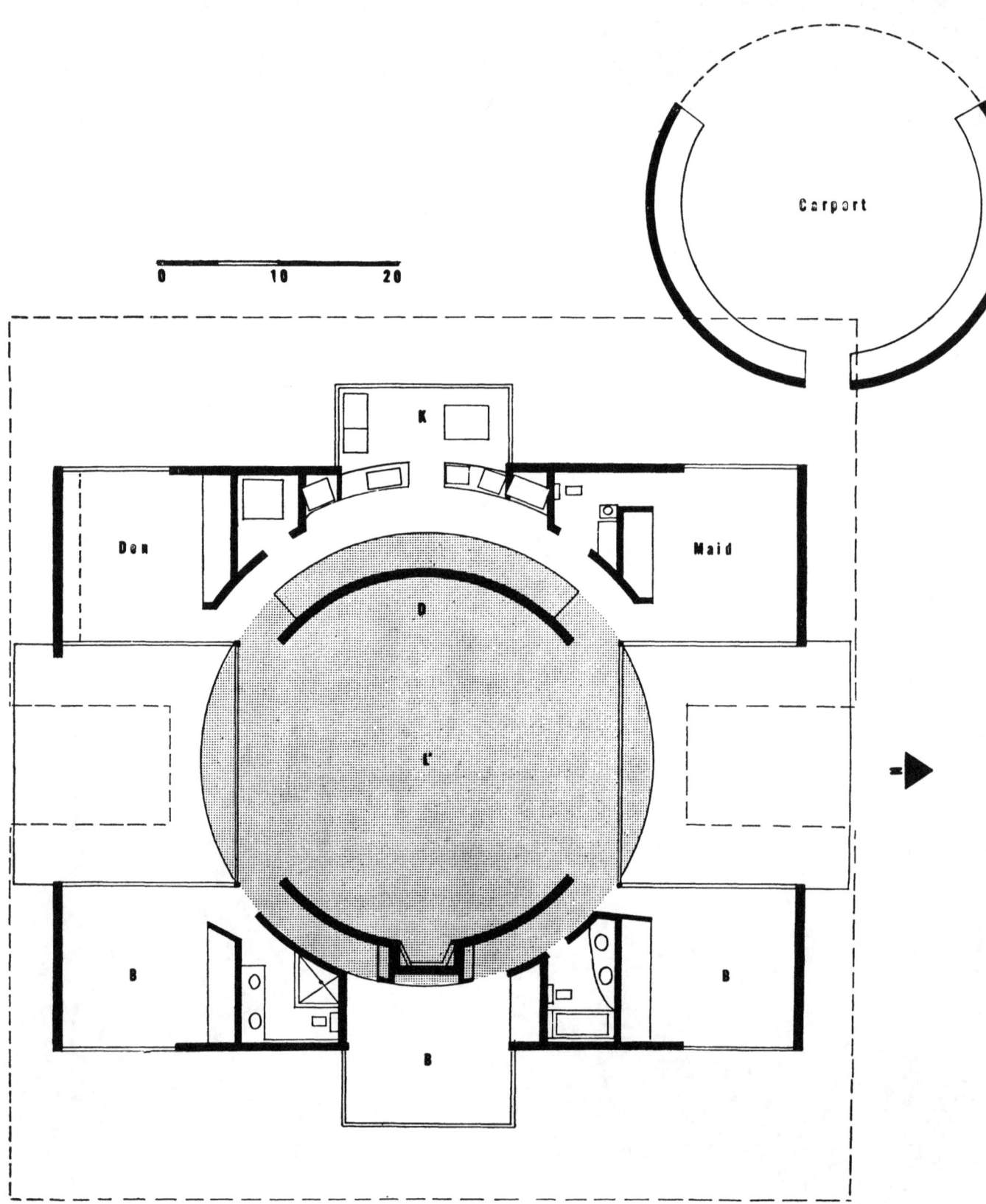

*Plate V*

Plate I                                             Tennessee Valley Authority

For total architectural planning and execution the Tennessee Valley Authority is unique in the history of the world. Although many books have been and will be written about it, the few illustrations here shown will at least indicate its magnitude. It was begun in 1933 and was accomplished in one generation by the democratic method of cooperation between a public corporation representing the federal government and possessed of the initiative of private enterprise and the people of the great watershed which lies in Virginia, Tennessee, North Carolina, Georgia, Alabama, Mississippi, and Kentucky. The nine dams impounding large lakes and

*Plate II*

the series of seventeen tributary dams and lakes of the whole complex have changed 40,910 square miles of denuded terrain and silt-filled rivers "too thick to swim in and too thin to plow" back into a rich magnification of what had originally been there. Substandard housing, low yield crops, and many other evidences of poverty were characteristic of many parts of the Valley. The reclamation planning and execution not only changed this but compounded the benefits with increased recreation facilities, abundant and inexpensive electricity, new forests, total flood control and new industries. An example of TVA-planned housing developments is shown in Plate I, Norris, Tennessee, which grew from the necessity of providing housing for fifteen hundred men engaged in building Norris Dam. It was conceived as a permanently small town within easy reach of the urban network of Knoxville, Tennessee, and its physical planning was based on Ebenezer Howard's "garden city" green-belt system. Near the little town, on the Clinch River is Norris Dam, Plate II. This picture was made looking upstream from near the right abutment. Plate III, the powerhouse of Gallatin Steam Plant near Gallatin, Tennessee, demonstrates the twentieth-century wedding of form and function in TVA plants. Its four units have a generating capacity of 1,050,000 kilowatts. Plate IV is a visitors' building near Boone Dam, Kingsport, Tennessee. The beautiful Kingston Steam Plant near Kingston, Tennessee, Plate V, generates 1,600,000 kilowatts.

*Plate III*

Plate IV

*Plate V*

Plate VI

Plate I

Nashville, Tennessee, is a typical example of a so-called "modern" Southern city decaying at its central core while spreading its urban sprawl ever outward to eat up new land. In the state where TVA successfully achieved most of the goals of regional planning, it is significant to see that the capital city is one of the region's leaders in using drastic architectural surgery to cut out the dead tissue of its core. It has adopted a land-use plan that will not only augment healthy growth, in the areas being redeveloped, but, with proper future control, will also help in affecting a gradual revitalization of the whole region. The Nashville Housing Authority administers several redevelopment projects. The furthest along is the renewal of

*Plate II*

capitol hill (Plate II). The entire capitol site (Plate I) was surrounded by urban rot, and the planners found that it was best to relocate completely the capitol's adjoining slum dwellers and to use the land for government buildings, parks, and healthy business and professional growth. The whole area is being linked into a new city and interstate traffic system with a peripheral loop around the capitol and central business section. Important features of this plan are that the displaced citizens are being moved to clean residential areas and that a strict architectural control system has already been set up on capitol hill to guard and protect future land use. The Nashville projects are being financed by federal funds, local grants-in-aid, and by private capitol from land purchases. The tax base on the capitol hill project will be considerably raised so that it will return to producing revenues rather than liabilities. This increase will help to pay the government loans. (*Clarke, Rapuano, and Holleran, Architectural Consultants, in conjunction with The Nashville Housing Authority.*)

# *Index*

Aalto, A., 7
Adams, Richard J., 80, 81
Adelphi Terrace, 5
Aeck, Richard, & Associates, 72, 73, 74, 75, 122, 132, 141, 150, 151
Alabama, 17, 163
Albers, Joseph, 149
Alexander, Cecil, 38, 39
Alexandria, Va., 28
America, 4, 5
America-Fore Insurance Group Building, New Orleans, La., 121
Amisano, Joseph, 65, 129, 130, 131
Architects Collaborative, Architects, 82, 83
Associated Building, Columbia, S.C., 125
Atlanta, Ga., 38, 39, 77, 132
Atlantic Christian College, Wilson, N.C., 45
Augusta, Ga., 14
Aydelott, A. L., & Associates, 64, 96, 97, 123

Baltimore, Md., 4
Barnes, Miller D., 38, 39
Barron, C. Errol, 78, 79
Barron, Heinberg & Brocato, 78, 79
Bath, England, 5
Baton Rouge, La., 34, 35, 142, 147
Bauhaus, 7, 143
Bayou LaFourche, La., 98, 99
Beaux Arts, 7
Bee Ridge Presbyterian Church, Sarasota, Fla., 141, 153, 154, 155, 156, 157
Bertoia, Harry, 153
Biggs, Thomas Jones, 60, 61
Biggs, Weir & Chandler, 60, 61
Birmingham, Ala., 6
Bissett, Thomas Jefferson, 68, 125, 128
Boaz, Joseph N., 117, 118, 119, 120, 169
Bontura House, Natchez, Miss., 20
*Book of Architecure*, 4
Boston, Mass., 4
Bristol, Tenn., 96, 97
British, 4
Brocato, Joseph M., 78, 79
Brunswick, Ga., 14
Bunshaft, Gordon, 148, 149

California, 3, 8, 46, 106
Calongne, William F., Jr., 31
Caribbean, 4
Carib Building, New Orleans, La., 112, 113
Carlisle, William Aiken, 68, 125, 128
Cartersville, Ga., 122
Casa Merieult, New Orleans, La., 15
Catalano, Eduardo, 152
Candela, Felix, 141
Chandler, Sydney W., 60, 61
Charleston, S.C., 3, 4, 6, 13, 18, 19
Charlotte, N.C., 86, 87, 88, 89, 90, 91, 92
Charlottesville, Va., 11
Chattanooga, Tenn., 129, 130, 131
Christian Brothers College, Memphis, Tenn., 64

Civic Center, New Orleans, La., 108
Civic center, Tallahassee, Fla., 82, 83
Civil War, 6, 20
Clarke, Gilmore D., 170, 171
Classroom Building, North Carolina State College, Raleigh, N.C., 144, 145, 146
Clemson, S.C., 8, 68
Clemson College, Clemson, S.C., 57
Cleveland, Ohio, 6
Colbert, Charles R., 133
Coliseum for Georgia Institute of Technology, Atlanta, Ga., 72, 73, 74, 75
College Union, North Carolina State College, Raleigh, N.C., 62
Columbia, S.C., 125, 128
Columbus, Ga., 14
Conover, N.C., 100, 101, 102, 103
Continent, The, 4
Cooper River, 18
Corinthian, 21
Cotton Exchange Building, 24
Cotton gin, 122
Courthouse, Montgomery, Ala., 84
Coventry, 6
Curtis, Nathaniel Cortlandt, Jr., 32, 36, 37, 46, 47, 76, 93, 94, 95, 112, 113, 121, 126, 127
Curtis & Davis, 32, 36, 37, 46, 47, 76, 93, 94, 95, 112, 113, 121, 126, 127

Daniel, Robert W., house, Knoxville, Tenn., 42
Davis, Arthur Q., 32, 36, 37, 46, 47, 76, 93, 94, 95, 112, 113, 121, 126, 127
Deitrick, William Henley, 62, 104, 105
*Designs of A. Palladio*, 4
De Soto Hotel, Savannah, Ga., 6, 24
Dinemountain, Ga., 141, 150, 151
Drive-in-bank, Raleigh, N.C., 114, 115, 116
Dudok, Willem, 7

Eastgate Shopping Center, Chattanooga, Tenn., 129, 130, 131
Edgehill, Va., 12
Edwards, George, house, Charleston, S.C., 13
Edwards, H. Griffith, 77
Edwards & Portman, 77
Egyptian, 6
Elstad, Eivind G., 104, 105
England, 4
English, 4, 5, 20, 106
Englishmen, 3

FHA, 9
Federal, 5
Filling station, Garner, N.C., 134
Finch, Alexander, Barnes, Rothschild & Paschal, 38, 39
Finch, James H., 38, 39
Fitzgibbon, James W., 42, 147
Florida Southern College, Lakeland, Fla., 57, 58, 59
Fredericksburg, Va., 12
Freedman town house, New Orleans, La., 30, 31
French, 3, 4, 20
Fuller, Buckminster, 141, 147

Gallatin Steam Plant, Gallatin, Tenn., 165
Gallatin, Tenn., 165
Georgia, 16, 24, 163
Georgia Institute of Genetics, Cartersville, Ga., 122
Georgia Institute of Technology, Atlanta, Ga., 7
Georgian, 3, 5, 9, 15, 25, 36
Germany, 7, 8
Gibbs, 4
Goodman, Charles M., 28
Gothic, 93
Gothic Revival, 5, 6
Greek, 7
Greek Revival, 5, 21
Gregory Poole Equipment Co., Raleigh, N.C., 136
Gulf Coast, 107
Gulf of Mexico, 4, 5, 21, 113

Harkey residence, Pascagoula, Miss., 36
Harlan Memorial Hospital of the Miner's Memorial Hospital Association, Harlan, Kentucky, 80, 81
Harmon, G. Thomas, III, 66, 67
Hayes, Thomas T., Jr. & Associates, 63
Heinberg, Max J., 78, 79
Herron house, Sarasota, Fla., 158, 159, 160, 161, 162
Hogansville, Ga., 22
Holland, 7
Holloway, John, 144, 145, 146
Howard, Ebenezer, 165
Hughes, David, 148, 149
Huguenots, 4

Italian Renaissance, 5, 7

Jamestown, Va., 142
Jefferson, Thomas, 10, 11, 149
Jeffersonian, 4, 9
Johnson, Philip, 7
Johnston, Frances B., 14

Kamphoefner, Henry L., 27
Kansas City, Mo., 106
Keenan, William J., III, 66, 67
Kensington, 5
Kentucky, 163
Knoxville, Tenn., 42
Krueger, Max, 104, 105

Lamm, 11
Lawrence, John W., 31
Lawrence, Saunders & Calongne, 31
Le Corbusier, 7, 149
Leoni, 4
Library, Natchitoches, La., 78, 79
Library, New Orleans, La., 76
Lincoln's Inn, 5
Livestock Judging Pavilion, Raleigh, N.C., 104, 105
London, 5
Louisiana, 32
Louisville, Ga., 16
Lundy, Victor, 137, 138, 139, 140, 141, 153, 154, 155, 156, 157, 158, 159, 160, 161, 162
Lutheran Church, Conover, N.C., 100, 101, 102, 103
Lyles, Bissett, Carlisle & Wolff, 68, 125, 128
Lyles, William Gordon, 68, 125, 128

Macon, Ga., 14
Madison Ave., 6
Married Student Housing Units, Raleigh, N.C., 63
Masonic Temple, Charleston, S.C., 19
Matsumoto, George, 40, 41, 136
Medical Building, Atlanta, Ga., 77
Mediterranean, 5, 17
Meir, Ezra, house, Raleigh, N.C., 152

Memphis, Tenn., 3, 6, 123
Merrill, John O., 148, 149
Methodists, 9
Milledgeville, Ga., 14
Mississippi, 5, 163
Mississippi Hospital School, Jackson, Miss., 60, 61
Mobile, Ala., 3, 17, 21
Montgomery, Ala., 23, 84
Moses Building, Montgomery, Ala., 23
Motel de Ville, New Orleans, La., 133
Murrell, G. Ross, Jr., 34, 35

Narrows, Parker Alfred, 84
Nashville Housing Authority, 169, 170
Nashville, Tenn., 169, 170
Natchez, La., 3, 20
Navajo, 27
Nervi, Pier Luigi, 141
New Deal, 142
New Orleans, La., 3, 5, 6, 15, 17, 20, 30, 46, 69, 76, 108, 112, 113, 121, 126, 127, 133, 142
New World, 4
New York, N.Y., 4
Nichols, F. D., 14
Niemeyer, Oscar, 107
Norris, Tenn., 163, 164
North Carolina, 8, 43, 163
North Carolina State Board of Education, 8
North Carolina State College, Raleigh, N.C., 7, 8, 124, 144, 145, 146, 147
North Carolina Superintendent of Public Instruction, 8
Nowicki, Matthew, 104, 105
Nurses' home and school, Bristol, Tenn., 96, 97

Odell, A. G., & Associates, 48, 49, 50, 86, 87, 88, 89, 90, 91, 92, 100, 101, 102, 103
Office and apartment building, Memphis, Tenn., 123
Oglethorpe, 6, 24
Oglethorpe University, Atlanta, Ga., 65
Oliver, Louis Arthur, 54, 55, 56
Oliver & Smith, 54, 55, 56
Oud, J. J. P., 7
Owings, Nathaniel, 148, 149

Palladian, 141
Palladio, A., 4, 7, 21
*Palladio Londinensis,* 4
Paris, 6
Parking deck, Atlanta, Ga., 132
Parthenon, 7
Pascagoula, Mississippi, 36
Paschal, Caraker D., 38, 39
Pavilion Restaurant, Dinemountain, Ga., 141, 150, 151
Pearson, Clyde Collins, 84
Pearson, Tittle & Narrows, 84
Pediatric Clinic, Bayou LaFourche, La., 98, 99
Philadelphia, Pa., 4, 6, 17
Picasso, Pablo, 149
Piggly-Wiggly, Garner, N.C., 135
Pittsburgh, Pa., 6, 108
Portman, John C., Jr., 77
Presbyterians, 8
Preston, William Gibbons, 24
Princess Anne County High School, Va., 54, 55, 56
PWA, 8, 43

Raleigh, N.C., 27, 40, 62, 63, 114, 115, 116, 124, 136, 141, 144, 145, 146, 152
Rapuano, Michael, 170, 171
Raymond Loewy & Associates, 109, 110, 111
Reeves, Ralph, 144, 145, 146
Renaissance, 4
Reynolds Aluminum Building, Richmond, Va., 141, 148, 149

Richardson, H. H., 6, 24
Richmond, Va., 3, 6, 141, 149
Rich's Department Store, Knoxville, Tenn., 109, 110
Riverview High School, Sarasota, Fla., 51, 52, 53
Roman Catholic Church, 69
Romanesque, 6
Roosevelt, Franklin D., 6
Rothschild, Bernard B., 38, 39
Rotunda, 11
Royston, Robert N., 109, 110, 111
Rudolph, Paul, 51, 52, 53

Saarinen, Eliel, 7
St. Augustine, Fla., 3, 142
Salmon, 4
Samuels, A., 21
Samuely, Felix James, 141
Sarasota, Fla., 137, 153, 154, 155, 156, 157, 158, 159, 160, 161, 162
Saunders, George A., 31
Savannah, Ga., 3, 4, 5, 6, 14, 15, 24
Sawyer, Raymond, 135, 136, 144, 145, 146
Scandinavia, 7
School of Design, 8, 147
Severud, Fred N., 104, 105
Severud-Elstad-Krueger, Engineers, 104, 105
Sherlock, Chris J., 80, 81
Sherlock, Smith & Adams, 80, 81
Short, Sam B., Jr., 34, 35
Short & Murrell, 34, 35
Shushan house, Harahan, La., 32
Skidmore, Louis, 148, 149
Skidmore, Owings and Merrill, 148, 149
Slave Market, Louisville, Ga., 16
Small, G. Milton, 85, 117, 118, 119, 120, 124, 136, 169
Small & Boaz, 117, 118, 119, 120, 169
Smith, Herbert L., III, 54, 55, 56
Smith, Moreland Griffith, 80, 81
South Carolina, 4
South Carolina National Bank, Columbia, S.C., 128
Southerner, 3, 8, 10, 25
Spanish, 3, 4, 20
Stevens, Preston S., 109, 110, 111
Stevens & Wilkinson, 109, 110, 111
Stone, Edward D., 66, 67
Stuart, Duncan R., 147
Sullivan, Louis, 6, 7, 23, 24, 62, 106
Sustan Garment Factory, New Orleans, La., 126, 127
Synergetics Incorporated, 147

TV, 107
Tallahassee, Fla., 142
Tennessee, 163
Tennessee Valley Authority, 142, 163, 164, 165, 166, 167, 168
Thomy Lafon School, New Orleans, La., 46
Tittle, Farrow Lee, 84
Toombs, Amisano & Wells, 65, 129, 130, 131
Toombs, Henry Johnston, 65, 129, 130, 131
Tulane University, New Orleans, La., 8

Unitank, Baton Rouge, La., 142, 147
United Mine Workers, 70
United States, 3
University of South Carolina, Columbia, S.C., dormitories for men, 66, 67
University of Virginia, Charlottesville, Va., 11

Van Der Rohe, Ludwig Mies, 3, 7, 141
Venturi, 12
Victorian, 5, 6, 7, 21, 23, 24
Vieux Carré, 5, 31
Virginia, 4, 163
Virginia Museum of Fine Art, Richmond, Va., 149
Vitruvius, 26, 62
*Vitruvius Scoticus*, 4

WRAL-TV, Raleigh, N.C., 117, 118, 119, 120
Wake Forest College, Winston-Salem, N.C., 9
Warm Mineral Springs Inn, Sarasota, Fla., 137
Washington, D.C., 3, 9
Waugh, Edward W., 85, 135, 136, 144, 145, 146
Waugh & Sawyer, 135, 136, 144, 145, 146
Weidlinger, Paul, 141
Weir, Harry Edmiston, 60, 61
Wells, James Edwin, 65, 129, 130, 131
West Indies, 4
Wijdeveld, H. Theodorus, 7
Wilkinson, James R., 109, 110, 111
Williams, Edward, 109, 110, 111
Williams, F. Carter, 114, 115, 116
Williamsburg, Va., 3
Wilson Junior High School, Mecklenburg County, N.C., 48, 49, 50
Wilson, N.C., 169
Winston-Salem, N.C., 9, 85
Wolff, Louis Michael, 68, 125, 128
World War II, 7, 28, 106
Wren, Christopher, 6
Wright, Frank Lloyd, 3, 6, 7, 22, 24, 57, 58, 59, 143, 149

www.ingramcontent.com/pod-product-compliance
Lightning Source LLC
Chambersburg PA
CBHW081820300426
44116CB00014B/2433